t

VIEW

from

13F

ONE WOMAN'S
STORY OF SURVIVING
FLIGHT 811

Shari Peterson

The View From 13F: One Woman's Story of Surviving Flight 811
Published by Good Egg Publishing Network.
Denver, CO

ISBN: 978-0-578-53121-2
Personal Memoir / Survival

Gratitude to:

    Front Cover and interior design by Victoria Wolf
    Back cover design by Matt Merki
    Editor and writing coach, Bobby Haas
    Publishing Consultant, Polly Letofsky with My Word Publishing
    Author photo, Jenn Hernandez
    English Teacher, Alburnett High School, Mrs. Betenbender

QUANTITY PURCHASES: Schools, companies, professional
groups, clubs, and other organizations may qualify for special
terms when ordering quantities of this title. For information, email
shari@sharipetersonauthor.com.

AUTHOR'S NOTE

This book is my story and to the best of my recollection the events
shared in this book are as they occurred. Many of the people
in this book are named, with their permission, and a few of the
names have been changed to protect their privacy.

Heidi-Ho and Big Tuna
We Did It!

who doesn't love
a turtle with
a top hat?

Chapter One

A HAWAIIAN SUNRISE ON ANY DAY is a mystical and breathtaking experience.

On the morning of February 24, 1989, the clear, starry night slowly gave way to the predawn tranquility of a tropical sunrise. Outdoors, a hush encompassed the island as exotic birds softly called to each other; mild ocean breezes rustled palm trees, while gentle surf slapped against the pristine Hawaiian sand beaches.

Alone in a small sequestered area of the vacant and strangely silent Honolulu United Airlines' Red Carpet Room, I was numb and groggy. Curled up in a semi-fetal position on the worn lounge-area sofa, I clung to my only comforts, a small regulation size airline pillow and child-size, lightweight airline blanket.

Grateful the sun was finally beginning to break through the predawn gloom that both paralyzed and comforted me, I slowly shook my head to clear the brain fog. My entire body shuddered as my jumbled thoughts returned to that one moment in time. "What the hell just happened?"

Staring out, my thoughts looped in disbelief as unexpected waves of wonder, awe, and gratitude crashed into my brain. Startled at these emotions, my mind paused to ponder the enormity of the reality that I was even alive to see this morning's sunrise. Watching the scene in front of me slowly shift from darkness to daybreak, my breath caught as I silently communicated my gratitude, "Thank you, God, for letting me see the light of this new day."

Closing my eyes to hold back tears, it felt as though Mother-Vic joined me in my thoughts. My awareness drifted to her and her common sense when a tough day ended. A slight smile crept onto my tired face as I imagined her sitting next to me, watching this particular sunrise, musing, "I wonder what this day will bring?"

Another shudder and sigh snapped me back to the present; I labored to comprehend the inconceivable recent events. In a feeble attempt to at least gain some sliver of understanding, I sifted through everything I thought I knew, yet remained stuck on, "What the hell just happened here …?"

Sighing deeply, gripping the blanket to pull it tighter around my shoulders, I willed myself to fully sit up.

Muffled sounds in the large lounge area signaled staff and officials had begun quietly moving about, trying not to disturb the dozen or so of us who were sequestered and spent the night in the various corners of the makeshift sleeping accommodations.

Reliving the blurred past several hours, my mind reeled with the unimaginable memories of the explosion, the chaos, the crippled landing, the cacophony of rapid-fire questions that came from all directions.

Suddenly crashing back into my focus were the questions from the concerned medical staff on the tarmac, "Are you injured? Where? Are you needing medical assistance? Medications? Glasses? Hearing aids? Do you need to see a doctor? Do you need to get to a hospital?"

Then, once inside the terminal, feeling dazed and bombarded with even more questions from airline employees, "Are you OK? What do you need? What did you see/hear/smell?"

In the midst of this bedlam, other United 811 passengers were transported from the tarmac to the airport terminal, where emergency crews and first responder personnel escorted them to the hastily set up interrogation area.

The commotion raged around us as countless people ran by, shouting instructions; emergency vehicles rushed past with flashing lights and sirens blaring. Someone in charge took me by the arm to start a queue near the small pay phone bank lining the wall of the concourse so we could contact loved ones.

Only a few hours ago, the FBI and airline representatives had separated the small handful of us seated in the business class section from the other passengers, taking us from the chaos on the tarmac and escorting us to the Red Carpet Room.

The remaining passengers were herded into the terminal and accommodations set up in a large open space against a terminal wall. One thin line of hastily draped bright yellow police tape was all that separated more than 300 stunned United 811 passengers from the gawking public and other airline passengers going about their own business.

Federal agents in their dark blue jackets with a bold FBI logo on the back briskly moved me to a small private area to conduct their witness interrogation. Several agents sat across from me and around me at a small, round table. The agent seated directly across asked the questions, watching intently as I tried my best to recall and answer.

Other agents seated close by watched me and my every move, "Who are you? Were you traveling with anybody—if so, who and where are they now? Where were you seated? Where was your seat in proximity to the explosion? What did you see? Did you hear anything suspicious? See anybody suspicious? Smell anything suspicious? Describe in detail exactly what happened."

Following the FBI questioning and debriefing, the team excused themselves. A new FBI team took their seats and began asking similar questions, to perhaps jar a fresh memory.

The controlled chaos of voices, commands, and questions bombarded me. Yet, my brain remained focused on one thing—there were people sitting in front of me and then they were gone.

After several hours of debriefing, another handler finally led me away to the relative quiet of the Red Carpet Room. There she offered food and drink, and the pillow, blanket, and sofa away from the adrenalin-charged pandemonium fueled by not only the incident but the ensuing confusion and din.

The new, sudden stillness provided a welcome oasis of quiet and some time for me to finally be alone with my thoughts.

A seasoned traveler, I simply could not get my head around the surreal scene all around me. Taking another deep breath, my body shuddered as my thoughts could only return and repeatedly attempt to process, "What the hell just happened here?"

Sitting quietly, alone, my thoughts far, far away, the night began to fade. My aching head lay on my crossed arms tightly hugging my knees. I focused on the distant faint outline of the aircraft nestled in the early dawn shadows.

The aircraft that only a few short hours ago had departed Honolulu on a routine flight to Auckland, then on to Sydney. The aircraft that not only nearly killed me but turned around, landed safely, and saved my life.

My breath caught as my brain abruptly registered, "I am not just now waking up from any dream or nightmare. This is real. This really did happen ..."

The sun's slow climb over the outline of the dark silhouette mimicked a curtain rising at the opening of a Broadway play.

The fuselage suddenly gleamed in the morning sun, the gaping hole on the right side fully exposed.

Gasping, my eyes fixated on the crippled airliner directly in my line of sight. My first daylight view of the devastation showed the damage was significant and obviously deadly.

Slowly the magnitude of the scene unfolding before me became crystal clear.

From that day forward, my life was forever changed.

Chapter Two

GROWING UP IN IOWA
LATE 1950S AND EARLY 1960S

WHEN I WAS A YOUNGSTER, maybe all of nine years old, I lazed away the days in the small pasture behind our Iowa farmhouse with Topsy, my Shetland pony.

Our family consisted of Mom (whom we affectionally called Mother-Vic), Dad, and my two younger sisters, Marilyn and Margaret (Madge), plus a variety of furry companions. Along with Topsy, we raised a few cows, pigs, a goat named Billy, bunny rabbits, farmyard dogs and cats, chickens, and eventually Pepper, a larger pony we purchased after I grew too big to ride Topsy.

Home was our rented older, classic styled two-story farmhouse with a large, slightly dilapidated covered front porch. Front porches were common on homes of that era, and ours faced the dirt road that lead to the nearest small community, Toddville, Iowa.

Toddville was not a town you visited; you either lived there or were simply passing through. A mere speck on the Iowa map, Toddville was accessed via dusty, gravel roads leading from the highway. It boasted a Legion Hall, grade school, small apartment house, the Methodist church, and a tiny post office, plus the population at the time of maybe 60 – 80 residents. There were no paved streets, streetlights, or sidewalks, and the only business was a small general store that closed many years ago.

The main family entry into the house was through the smaller and much-used side porch, which also offered easy access to the outdoor wood pile for our wood burning heat. Entering the side porch put you directly into the large farm-style kitchen area. The kitchen was the heart of the house and where we would usually find Mother-Vic as she prepared meals and waited for us to come home at the end of the day.

An ancient laminate-topped, shiny, grooved, aluminum-edged kitchen table in the middle of the kitchen was the cornerstone and the catchall to drop our belongings as we passed through on the way upstairs to change into play clothes. Lingering at the table while we were unloading our things, some freshly baked sweet treat would catch our eye. Later, we would clear the table, and this is where we sat together as a family for our meals.

In the summers, the side porch kitchen's wood-framed, creaky metal screen door continuously clanged shut behind us as we ran in and out of the house, shouting and laughing.

Our family of five thrived on this small, rural Toddville acreage. The timeworn white farmhouse, along with the two dilapidated, faded red barns and several smaller out-buildings were owned by Lloyd, a local farmer, and his wife, Wilma. Lloyd was a former railroader with Dad, and after Lloyd semiretired from the railroad, he often dropped by to play cribbage, deliver some morning fresh milk and cream, or just discuss "life."

DAD WAS PHILLIP "PHIL" J. PETERSON, a lanky six-foot-two, 100 percent Norwegian descendant and decorated WWII Marine.

By age seventeen, this long-limbed, street smart young man evolved into a tough combat veteran who was awarded the Purple Heart and a Bronze Star for his service.

Following in the footsteps of his hearty railroader father, Henry, Dad worked his way up to an engineer position with the Chicago Northwestern Railroad. The engineer of the train crew is responsible for the actual operation of the locomotive, and this type of work required long hours, often in difficult Midwest hot, humid summers or bitter, bone-chilling cold, brutal winter weather.

Dad was often on call and there were seldom regularly scheduled days off. With little notice from dispatch, he would be directed to report in for jobs which took him out of town to move trains all over the Midwest. Typically, he was gone for several days at a time.

As much as he enjoyed his work out on the road, he loved being home, where he would putter around the property with the ever-present screwdriver and a pair of pliers sticking out the back pocket of his worn, faded blue overalls. Or he would tackle a project in his garage workshop, maybe a paint project, chopping wood for our winter heat, or repairing a vehicle.

Between dropping out of school in the seventh grade and joining the Marines at seventeen, Dad would wander. He would climb on board his prized Harley-Davidson motorcycle and hit the road to California or parts unknown. He also worked as an automotive mechanic and briefly co-owned a small local gas station and vehicle repair shop. He gave all this up to fight overseas.

While vehicle repair was no longer his livelihood, he loved to get under the hood of any jalopy and tinker with the engine or spend his time keeping them spotless.

In his orderly world, clean cars were a must. If we were organizing a trip to town and there was no time to tidy up the entire vehicle, Dad would make certain at least the auto's wheels and rims were pristine.

Most people simply jump in the car, start it up, and drive away. Nope. It did not matter the weather conditions, he would, at the very least, hose off the dirt and then carefully dry the wheels before we left the driveway.

Even if it was simply the short drive to Toddville Sunday School, we would watch and laugh as he washed the wheels in a cold rain before driving the three miles to the church and back. He chuckled as well, but we all knew it was important to him.

While Dad puttered with his cars, we played in the garage or in the dirt near him. Times like these were a perfect opportunity for this funny man to create and spin grand stories. Dad's imaginative tall tales often revolved around his "fantasy" days of playing professional football or wrestling professionally on TV, weighing in at 300 pounds. Maybe the tale that day would be whizzing around the skating rink during his roller derby skater days, skating on the same team as "The Blonde Bomber," the great Joanie Weston, or playing professional basketball with Wilt Chamberlin and teaching Wilt how to shoot a hook shot. Another time, he might point toward the moon and describe his moon walks. All his tales were told with great detail and sincerity.

He honed his storytelling skills at every opportunity. After supper, he would call for us to draw us out of the kitchen and give Mother-Vic breathing room to clean up the kitchen without our "help."

His voice was like a dog whistle to us. We perked up and scurried over to him like a litter of puppies, scampering over each other, giggling, until we found spots on his lap. Following this commotion, the three of us would finally settle in, look up at his smiling face, as he began,

"Hey, did I ever tell you about the time ..."

Years later, I learned Mother-Vic would listen from the kitchen; sometimes, she would peek around the corner and stifle her giggles as even she couldn't believe the enormity of his many fantastical feats. She would stop mid-task to listen and try hard not to laugh out loud as she watched us, silent, focused, listening intently, eyes opened wide, completely mesmerized as he described in fascinating detail his new moon friends, their pets, and what they really ate on the moon—according to him, it was not green cheese.

EIGHT MONTHS OUT of the year, clean cars topped Dad's important to-do list. However, during the four summer months, tending his enormous garden moved to the top of that list.

Our family subsisted on what we grew and preserved during the summer. Produce from the garden, plus Lloyd's fresh milk and the fresh eggs, chicken, pork, and beef from our pasture functioned as our simple and nutritious diet. We didn't eat exotic avocados or pineapples—if it didn't grow in Iowa, we had no reason to try it.

Dad's pride in his picture-perfect garden was well deserved. He spent hours tilling, turning and working the soil. Once he had made the soil ready to his satisfaction, he set small branches found around the property into the ground at both ends of each row; then he would run string down each row, securing the string to the grounded branch. These became his markers to ensure he planted the rows straight as an arrow and they were perfectly spaced.

We would watch and learn as he patiently talked gardening while he meticulously planted seeds and small plants in their places to begin their growing season. As we grew older, he "let us" help with this spring ritual.

He planted peas, green beans, sweet corn, tomatoes, strawberries, rhubarb, and mostly potatoes, hills and hills of potatoes. His favorite potato was the Kennebec, a commonly grown white potato. One year, he estimated he put 800 pounds of his Kennebec's in the cellar.

Yes, we ate a lot of potatoes—fried potatoes with breakfast, boiled potatoes with most every meal, and a treat around our house was when he made a batch of Kumla, a Norwegian family tradition made with, yup, potatoes.

Kumla is made by first hand grinding the peeled potatoes. The Kumla making process began when Mother-Vic anchored the ancient food grinder to the edge of the kitchen table. When she brought out this grinder, or the "Kumla crusher" as we called it, we knew we were in for a feast! Not many non-Norwegians developed a taste for Kumla. It is most certainly a rib-sticking food, good for the Norwegian soul after being out on a cold, windy, winter day tending chores.

Dad would start with the ground potatoes, then he mixed that with flour, salt, and pepper. He would skillfully form a handful of the mixture into balls that were slightly smaller than a baseball but larger than a golf ball. After starting a kettle of simmering water, Dad added ham or ring baloney, then gently dropped the balls into that kettle of water, covered it, and let it cook slowly.

After about an hour or so, he used our designated spoon, or "Kumla scoop," to remove one or two of the balls from the simmering kettle to our plate. The anticipation was enormous as we cut and sliced the steaming potato balls, added lots of butter, salt, and pepper, and a small piece of the simmered meat alongside. The more butter, the better! Yes, to this day, Kumla on a cold winter day is still a delight.

Iowa's hot summer months of July and August often found Dad standing in the garden with his watering hose, watering and talking to the plants while he pulled those pesky weeds.

Often a harmless garter snake would slither from beneath the cool, shaded undergrowth of the growing plants. Even though garter snakes are only fifteen to twenty inches long, they can certainly startle someone picking through the plants for fresh peas or beans. When discovered, the snake often quickly moved away, but sometimes, and so much worse occasionally, the picker happened to grab one! There would be a gasp and/or a small scream and a toss of the snake to the other side of the garden. Then a deep breath and carry on!

In the fall, Dad began the hard work of harvesting the bounty and digging up the freshly grown potatoes. He scooped the potatoes out of the hills where they spent the summer growing. Our job was to take the fresh-dug potatoes, clean the dirt off, and haul them down into our cool cellar for winter storage.

You get the picture—Dad was not one to spend any of his precious family time sitting in front of the TV, unless his University of Iowa Hawkeyes were playing football.

Before televised college football games, Dad listened to the Iowa Big Ten games on a dusty, small, brown, 1940s-style radio in the garage.

Radio play by play in the 1950s and early 1960s was wonderfully colorful, with the crowd noise and the college marching bands, plus the enthusiasm and voice tones of the announcers setting the scene.

When there was excitement, we stopped what we were doing, stared intently at the radio, and effortlessly envisioned the players making passes, blocks, tackles, and running plays. Following a significant play, touchdown, or a move of the chains for an Iowa first down, Dad would throw his hands up into the air and dance around while sing-songing, "First and ten, do it again!" as he explained the game he loved so much.

LIVING IN THE COUNTRY, we seldom had visitors, so if the neighbors or kids came by, we would run to the door to see who wanted to play. Imagine our surprise the first time they asked if my dad could come out and play. A slow grin crossed his face, and he strode out the door, greeted by whoops and hollers from the kids. He would talk with them for a bit to see how everybody was doing, then maybe shoot baskets or organize a touch football game.

There was no boy/girl discrimination when we worked or played. We girls may have been in the field working next to the men during the day; then we would cleanup and put on a dress for a dance that evening. Where we grew up, you simply "showed up."

Playing football was an "all-in" neighborhood pastime. With a worn football as our only equipment, there were no jerseys, fancy shoes, or flags to grab to represent a tackle. Football plays were stopped with a tackle or by pushing the player out-of-bounds. As the game went on, it could get a little more physical, and the smaller kids would often remove themselves from the field as a way to stay in one piece.

Boy or girl, if you were tackled or knocked down and did not immediately get right back up, my dad would stride over to assess the situation. Stopping, he would quickly look over the player, and if there was no significant damage, simply ask, "Ya in? Ya out?" That was his signal for the player to make up their mind—either get up and play or get yourself off the field.

Make no mistake, we were not coddled. When we fell down, no adult rushed over to pick us up and dust us off. We learned at a very young age to pick ourselves up, dust ourselves off, and to get back in the game, and we often played hurt.

Dad was smart, possessed a photographic memory, and was funny and frugal. We seldom disposed of anything we owned—we either passed it down within our immediate family or passed it along to another family; if anything we owned was damaged, Dad figured out a way to repair or repurpose it. He taught us great respect for the few things we had and to take care of the things we owned.

Many summer days were spent simply hanging out with him, tinkering on the car engines. When he was under the hood, my job was handing him tools and just talking. Often times, I overheard some slightly salty language when an uncooperative engine bolt didn't turn, something was stuck or out of reach. I learned simple life lessons from him when we washed and waxed cars, repaired a broken wagon cart, and tended to a proper cleanup after we repaired something. The rule was *always* clean your tools and immediately put them away— no exceptions. While these chores were a part of daily life, they were also significant learning experiences.

When anyone spent time with Dad, they could see he worked hard and made chores fun. Before he would tackle any project, he would first stand back to study the matter and simply ponder the situation in front of him. Me? I would be standing there, moving from foot to foot, impatient, ready to get this project started. I would show my frustration with the significant I-am-such-an-annoyed-kid sigh, "What are you dooooing?"

He would slowly turn, his hands in his pockets of his coveralls, and with a twinkle in his eye, slowly stretch out the words, "I'm meditating."

My dad relished a challenge; he was very good at solving difficult projects. Problem-solving and teamwork, plus having fun doing it? More great parental teaching, masquerading as chores.

As I look back, this was his time at the start of the task to go over the entire project in his head. He would apply his rational thinking of a three-dimensional chess player to study and then envision, "If I do this, what happens? If I fix it that way, what happens? I don't have that part/piece. What do I have, or what can I use instead of what I need? How can I make this work? How can I make this work better?"

Growing up, I only recall one story Dad shared about his childhood, and only through rare comments did we deduce it was less than ideal. When he was in the first grade, they had their usual "no Christmas" and on the first day back to school, his classmates would bring in the toy they received under the tree. He remembered his embarrassment from the previous year when he received nothing and had nothing to share. That next year, he asked a neighbor kid if he could "borrow" one small, carved wooden train car, which he then took to class to show what Santa brought him.

When I heard that story, I better understood why he was so excited when us kids had our Christmas and opened our presents. He was like a big kid too.

We did learn that in the seventh grade he was shown the door by his parents when they told him they could no longer afford to feed or take care of him. His only option was to pack his few belongings, and from then on, figure out how to take care of himself.

He never shared with us kids how he accomplished that, and I am sure that was part of the conversation during his lengthy first date with Mother-Vic.

As we grew older, we did learn that he and his two brothers, Bob and John, were local brawlers. Bob and John would stir something up, and then Dad stepped in to "clean up." Nobody in their small community wanted to mess with the Peterson Boys.

Dad was one of six children, three boys and three girls, Helen, Patty, and Norma Jean Peterson. The family moved often in and around the Randall, Iowa, area. Aunt Helen mused they lived in twenty-three houses by the time she graduated from high school.

From a very young age, and due to necessity, all the kids worked to support themselves. The girls hired out as housekeepers to cook and clean for local wealthier people—sometimes as live-in help. Working as young as ten years old, they handed over their earnings to their parents.

At seventeen, Dad joined the Marines. Seventeen sounds young, but by then, he had been on his own for about four years. He completed Marine basic training at Camp Pendleton in California before being whisked onto a Navy transport vessel for delivery to the front lines with the 3rd Battalion, 7th Marines, 1st Marine Division on October 9, 1943. Those brave Marines had been deployed to locate and destroy the enemy by fire and close combat. In short, they were there to fight.

Landing, he was immediately involved in several major battles of the Pacific Theatre.

Again and again, this regiment was called upon to storm the Japanese-held islands in the Pacific. He fought in Eastern New Guinea, New Britain, and the British Solomon Islands. "Bloody Peleliu" in the Palau Island Group is where he was awarded the Purple Heart for wounds he received there. During this deployment, he also suffered from malaria.

He saw intense fighting on the island fortress of Okinawa, where 1,200 Marines were killed or wounded. Here he was awarded the Bronze Star for heroic achievement.

His Bronze Star citation reads: "Corporal Peterson displayed exceptional initiative and leadership as a platoon guide during this period. When both the platoon commander and platoon sergeant became casualties, he assumed command and successfully led his platoon through the most difficult stages of the operation. His courage, determination, and complete disregard for his own personal safety were a constant inspiration to the men serving under him. Corporal Peterson's conduct, astute guidance, and unselfish devotion to duty reflect great credit upon himself and were in keeping with the highest traditions of the Marine Corps and the United States Naval Service."

At the conclusion of WWII, wounded and battle-weary, Dad returned to Iowa to pick up his life.

While Dad contended with his own demons relating to his service and battles during the war, he remained a humble, yet proud, Marine. He never spoke of this time and seldom shared stories with us. As children, we never saw his commendations; he kept them in a drawer somewhere. However, there were a handful of instances when he was troubled (today, it is identified as PTSD) when he reluctantly revealed brutal war stories, many he should probably not have shared with a little girl. One day, he explained the reason he didn't allow rice at our house was not only because we didn't grow it, but it also reminded him of the maggots on bodies from the casualties of war. It triggered a visceral response in him and a reminder that he lived, ate, and slept in the middle of all that carnage during the long battles—those soldiers from both sides that lay where they fell, exposed to the hot, humid Pacific sun, were the sights and smells surrounding the troops as they battled daily for their own lives.

However, he demonstrated great respect for the flag he fought to preserve and taught us flag etiquette. He remained adamant regarding our responsibilities as patriotic Americans and often reminded me that during WWII, he killed men every day so we could be free, use our voices, and never take our voting privileges for granted.

When Arthur "Bull" Jackson was awarded the Medal of Honor for his action on Peleliu in 1944, the citation mentioned a fellow Marine's contributions to that battle. That fellow Marine was my dad.

In 1990, Dad unexpectedly passed away at age sixty-five. He truly lived by the Marine motto of "Improvise, Adapt, and Overcome" and told me often as I was growing up to never, ever expect anybody to take care of me. "Figure it out," he said. That lesson served me well.

Semper Fi, Dad.

MOM WAS BORN Mildred LaVonne "Vicki" McVicker and was the youngest of five children. Their family of four girls, Rosie, Rene, Dory, Mom, and their brother, Larry "Bud" McVicker, grew up near Eagle Grove, Iowa.

The youngest and certainly the orneriest of her family, Mother-Vic shared stories of her deep insecurities and shyness during high school. After receiving a long, heartfelt pep talk letter from her brother, she took the bull by the horns and transformed.

After high school, she was first of her family to further her education at Coe College in Cedar Rapids. There she morphed from a shy schoolgirl into a dapper, shoe-collecting, fur-coat-wearing homecoming queen candidate and popular girl about campus.

Social work was her college focus, although due to

financial necessity, she left college prior to graduation to enter the workforce as a telephone operator in her hometown of Eagle Grove.

In the 1940s, the telephone company operator work environment was comprised of a long line of women in headsets seated in front of switchboards. These operators would answer incoming calls with, "Number, please?" then connect the phone call lines.

Throughout her early adult life, Mom worked off and on as a telephone operator. As small children, it was great fun to visit her there to watch the activity. Eventually, the telephone system evolved to a rotary dial system, which eliminated the need for live operators to connect every call.

When she left college to enter the workforce, she was single, dating, meeting people, attending dances, and very socially active. Some friends often mentioned they wanted to introduce her to this guy, Phil. She was busy with her life, her beaus, her work, and was just was not interested.

One Saturday night, she visited those friends to enjoy a casual evening. Sitting on the floor, playing with their new baby, she was wearing jeans and a flannel shirt; her hair wasn't "done," and she wore no makeup. This was not a good look back in the late 1940s, even for someone as confident and independent as Mother-Vic.

An unexpected knock at the door interrupted this fun evening and looking up, Mother-Vic watched, mesmerized, as this tall, fine-looking man wearing a sharp dark suit, bright white shirt, and tie entered the room. She recalled the minute he stopped in the doorway. His presence filled not only the doorway but the entire living room.

Mother-Vic was caught off guard as his strong gaze settled on her seated cross-legged on the floor holding the drooling baby. Without hesitation, he walked over to take the seat on the sofa next to her and introduced himself. So, this was "Phil."

They easily began talking and bantering. Time simply did not matter to either of them until they realized he had spent hours there and had stood up his date, just to get to know this woman.

Mother-Vic was absolutely horrified at her first impression in jeans, sitting on the floor. However, by the end of the evening, she agreed to a date with him, even though she was in the final stages of preparing to relocate to Omaha for another job and new scenery.

Their first date was for cocktails. Seated at the bar, talking and laughing, between the two of them, they ordered every drink on the menu board posted above the bar. Hours passed as Dad shared his life and experiences from the war, experiences that he had never told anyone else.

Mother-Vic forged ahead with her planned move to Omaha for her new telephone operator position. Yet, every other weekend, on his rare days off, Dad rode the train from Iowa to Omaha to see her.

This whirlwind romance meant they only spent two long weekends a month together over the next four months. That they then married after those four short months was extraordinary.

Mother-Vic often chuckled as she shared this story, saying he could have turned out to be "a real puke," but somehow it worked out. She often told us she would have married him and lived in a tent in a ditch. Why? Because the question wasn't if she could live with him; she realized she could not live without him.

Mom and Dad married on April 2, 1949, in front of a handful of family and friends in Aunt Dory's living room. Excited to start their family, I was born two years later.

Looking for adventure, Dad accepted a factory job in Los Angeles with Lockheed Martin and packed the three of us up to travel the two-lane highways from Iowa to Los Angeles.

Mother-Vic did not enjoy the long and sometimes unnerving drive in a packed car with a squirrely, restless, and curious infant. While Dad drove and she navigated, they tucked me out of the way in a cozy bed created in the back window of the 1950-era Ford.

The winter weather and treacherous road conditions they encountered on their drive through the Rocky Mountains, and especially over Colorado's Wolf Creek Pass, dictated a thirty-five mph top speed for a long portion of the drive.

Dad's work ethic and his "get 'er dun" attitude impressed the Lockheed bosses, but these Iowa-born and raised newlyweds missed their families, friends, and the Midwest lifestyle. Following a year living in Southern California, they decided it was time to pack up for a return trip back to Eagle Grove.

Old photos from that time showed us first resettled in a small trailer parked on Aunt Dory's Eagle Grove farm. From there, we lived in two different rental houses in Eagle Grove, and by then, my two sisters were in the picture.

Shortly after I completed the second grade in Eagle Grove, the railroad moved Dad to the Chicago area for a management position. He discovered that wearing a suit and shuffling papers in the office was not what he wanted and how much he missed being his own boss, outside and on the road.

Less than a year later, we left Illinois and returned to Iowa, settling into a small rental home located on the outskirts of Swisher, ten miles south of Cedar Rapids. We lived in Swisher less than a year before moving to Lloyd's farm property, approximately three miles out of Toddville, Iowa. From Lloyd's house, we moved and lived for a few years in a small house in the bedroom community of Midway, finally moving into a house located directly behind the school in Alburnett. This move eliminated most of the confusion of a one-car family transporting three teenagers to various, different school and church events for the next eight years. We lived there until we all graduated from Alburnett High School.

Together, their parenting style was far ahead of their time, and even their relationship was unlike most others we saw growing up. For fun, Dad's pet name for Mother-Vic was "the War Department." When we had a question or request, he would chuckle as he often directed us to her with, "Better check with the War Department about that."

Mother-Vic was not a typical 1950s homemaker, as she had little interest in cooking, cleaning, or handling domestic duties. She was much happier when she was playing and having fun. Independent, smart, kind, ridiculously generous, mischievous, musically talented, headstrong, adventurous, funny, and loyal, if she referenced someone as a "good egg," that was the highest compliment she could pay.

When irritated with somebody or something, she quickly assumed a brow-knitted, stern look and unleashed the don't-mess-with-me personality of a feisty, banty rooster. Unlike most 1950s housewives, she was confident and unafraid to speak up or stand her ground when she had something to say, believed something was not right or someone was being mistreated.

Back in the early 1950s, society dictated the man was the undisputed head of the household. However, what we witnessed was that Mother-Vic and Dad were equals who worked as a team on the household and in raising their three daughters.

Our parents believed in fewer parenting rules and more learning from the school of hard knocks. They would rather we had experiences to demonstrate "responsibility" and HOW to think, versus parental lectures about WHAT to think.

Whether we were playing, "feeding the chores" (our term for taking care of livestock), or helping one another with something, there was conversation, discussion, conflict resolution, the satisfaction of a job well done, and plenty of laughter, all core values of teamwork.

They easily demonstrated a sense of fairness in living their lives via their faith in the Golden Rule of treating people how you would want to be treated.

Every day, they gently coached us to be our best, mind our manners, say "please" and "thank you," and simple things, like staying seated at the dinner table until all were finished eating. They had zero tolerance for us kids using bad language, bullying, or name-calling. We were taught to always consider what other people were going through that we may not know about.

We were taught to recognize what our part or contribution was in any life situation and in difficult situations to ask ourselves, "What is the right thing to do here?" And also, to look for the humor in every encounter.

Here's an example of how that looked for me. When I was invited on my first date at fourteen, they gave me a suggested time to be home. After a couple of years, I had no curfew. Should I choose to return home late, I still remained responsible to get up early to start my day.

Having no curfew was unheard of in the early 1960s for a teenage girl, and it was all great until the morning when I realized it was no fun functioning on little sleep. My new choice was to arrive home earlier and get enough sleep, which sure made the next day go much better for me.

Because I was not operating under someone else's rule but rather by my own choice, there was no teen angst resulting in pushback from me, no drama or trying to lie or sneak around—no wasting my time thinking of ways to "trick the system" to stay out later. Rather, it was a valuable lesson in choices, personal responsibility, causes and effects.

I remember a lesson my sister Marilyn learned—it was cool to drive fast on the gravel back roads. However, that choice landed her, and Dad's car, in a ditch. She and the car were unharmed, and she realized she better have a plan to get it out and cleaned up because our parents were going to "let" her figure all that out and pay for it too.

After that speeding car experience and her stress getting herself out of it, Marilyn became a more responsible and careful driver next time she was allowed to drive the car.

She thought she pulled it off and they never knew, but years later, Dad said he found grass in the undercarriage in places it shouldn't be when he was washing the tires. Busted, but he never said a word to her, as he could see she was doing the appropriate things to make it right.

Dad often told us if we did something that ended up involving the law, under no circumstances should we expect them to bail us out. From very early on, whatever choices we made, we simply knew we were fully responsible for whatever effects that choice created. No exceptions.

Make no mistake, Dad and Mother-Vic were our biggest supporters. What they did not do was solve our growing up challenges by racing over with an open checkbook or my-kid-is-always-right attitude. We were far from perfect kids. We often made bad choices, and when asked, they helped us formulate a plan to work on the matter and sort it out. When we sisters fought, it was a doozy, but as we grew older, those sibling disagreements were few and far between.

However, as we moved into our teen and young adult years and were facing real difficulty, Dad, Mother-Vic, and my sisters were the first to help talk it out and sort out a solution. Because of those repeated lessons in taking responsibility for ourselves, Dad and Mother-Vic were confident and happy as each of us left home after high school. They were confident they had instilled the skills for us to, more often than not, make workable decisions and choices, unlike our other friends, who were going wild because they no longer had to live under someone else's rules. And they were happy because they were closer to an empty nest and their own time together.

Other than TV's 1950s generation of family shows such as *Father Knows Best, Leave It to Beaver,* and *The Donna Reed Show* as role models, I believed our childhood experiences were how everybody grew up.

I thank God often for their parenting and their lessons because I know I have the most fun with my family and that I can count on them when the chips are down, and having spent so much time together in both fun and difficult times, I trust them implicitly.

WHEN WE THREE GIRLS were around the ages of seven, five, and three, every two weeks on payday, Mother-Vic would round us up, clean us off, and take us on the fifteen-mile adventure all the way to Cedar Rapids on a grocery store run.

While we were fairly self-sufficient with our own food supplies, the grocery store carried the necessary toiletries, flour, sugar, and paper products, plus the rare treat of canned fruit cocktail or the extra special treat of a small box of breaded shrimp.

We three would "help" Mother-Vic audit the item selection to stay under her twenty dollar biweekly grocery budget. By reading labels, we learned new words and would ask her how to understand the label, peppering her with questions and just talking.

When our shopping was complete and the groceries safely stowed in the car, Mother-Vic would drive us to our next stop at the local Henry's, home of the fifteen-cent hamburger. There she would announce the amount of change left over from her twenty dollar budget. Our mission at Henry's was to work out what we could buy with the forty-six cents change or whatever amount remained.

We three would study the limited burger, fries, and soft drink menu as she helped us read the choices and discuss the options, plus do the numbers until we finally agreed on what appeared to be the best deal. Maybe that day it was one hamburger and two fries.

Mother-Vic would help us fairly split the food bounty between all of us. Not only was this great fun, it was another lesson in budgeting, as well as happily giving and sharing that which we had received.

Mother-Vic reminisced about a lesson she learned one day after she discovered extra grocery money change. She was expecting excited squeals as she shared the good news that there would be no "Henry's budget" that trip.

Because our lives were so strictly budgeted, she explained that meant we could buy whatever we wanted off their menu. She was taken aback by the silence and looks of disappointment on our faces. Puzzled by the lack of delight in this unexpected "treat," she realized that what we enjoyed and loved was the challenge of working together to figure out the best value for the loose change, and then we could share the fruits of our labor. That challenge and experience was what we treasured the most—*not* the food!

Years later, it remains funny how that theme repeated itself in our lives. It became so clear watching people work, sacrifice, strive for, and often choose the empty treat, versus enjoying the fulfilling experiences along the way to receiving the treat. It really *is* the journey, not the destination.

BEFORE THERE WERE ALL THESE kitchen gadgets, every meal was made from scratch—very little, if anything, was premade or served straight from the freezer. Potatoes were peeled, cooked, and mashed by hand, not using a mixer. The main meats and vegetables all started from raw, and at the end of the meal, pots, pans, dishes were handwashed, dried, and put away before the wife moved on to other household chores, such as ironing, darning, or helping with homework.

When Mother-Vic decided to bake a treat, it was a good idea to join her in the kitchen because some kind of fun was usually about to happen. One day, as she was getting her preparations ready to bake a cake, she was pulling the flour container from the cupboard when she looked at me with her naughty sideways grin.

She glanced to her right, then to her left, and mischievously swept her arm across the surface and started giggling as the flour flew off the table onto the floor.

Stomping her feet, she began swinging her arms and dancing. Flour was coming up like a cloud, and we began running around in the flour, making a mess and laughing like two very unruly, crazy people at the flour cloud, the flour all over our clothes, hair, and faces, the footprints all over the flour-covered kitchen. We were joyously making an unbelievable mess.

She often told us her philosophy was that we had only eighteen years to be her kids, so she was going to have fun with us during that short time. Little did we realize, as we grew up she became more than our mom, she also became our best friend. We laughed and played with her until she died in 2004, three weeks after her eightieth birthday party.

MOTHER-VIC'S SISTER, Aunt Dory, sold her Shetland pony, Topsy, to me for the grand sum of sixty dollars. Plus, for an additional ten dollars, she included his halter, bridle, and saddle. Seventy dollars total was big money for a nine-year-old in the early 1960s and would be about $615 in 2019 dollars.

So, with Mom and Dad's help, I worked out a financial plan to save that enormous seventy dollars sum by the following summer.

We agreed that rather than buying the school hot lunch, I would take my own school lunch, saving a dollar and fifty cents a week. We agreed to save my fifty cents of weekly milk money, and I would drink from the water fountain and have milk when I was home. Holiday gift cards and birthday cards often contained a one-dollar bill. Those rare cards I received that were holding two-dollars, or even five-dollar bills were equivalent to finding a gold nugget.

To find some additional revenue streams, I approached the nearby neighbors for any odd jobs. One neighborhood couple hired me to brush their horse for another fifty cents. One lady asked me to help her collect fresh eggs from the chicken coop, and I even picked up a few jobs watching a couple's smaller kids for a few hours. Every dime mattered in the Topsy fund-raising campaign. While the Topsy fund grew, we also factored in and deducted 10 percent of my earnings for tithing to our church. Dad and Mother-Vic did not suggest it; that was just what we did. I gladly set that 10 percent aside from every transaction.

My main focus during this time was not only finding ways to earn money, but I was also curious how to track all this activity. Mother-Vic and I often set aside time to sit at the kitchen table and empty the small mason jar I kept on top of my dresser that held all the carefully deposited coins and bills.

Counting the growing fund, she helped me learn how to keep track of my activities, while keeping my eye on the goal. The lessons started with her teaching me how to account for new funds collected, then doing the math to determine what amount was still required to reach the goal.

We would also stack the coins in the appropriate amounts in order to trade the coins for paper money. With all the serious accounting completed, the money would reverently be returned to the money jar and set back into its place on my dresser, where I continued to watch my dream grow.

Oh, the exhilaration when my seventy dollar total goal was reached by that next summer! Mother-Vic and Dad set it up with family members to make the transaction and transport Topsy the 150 miles from Aunt Dory's house in Eagle Grove to our home in Toddville.

When they told me Topsy would be delivered the next day, there was no sleeping that night. From my second-floor bedroom, I watched the moon slowly move across the sky as the gentle summer night breeze rustled the curtains in the open windows. Staring at the moon and then the ceiling, my mind was racing, dreaming of the adventures we would have and grateful for my family—thankful for their help making this dream really happen!

Rising early the next day and unable to sit still, I was counting the minutes until Topsy arrived. When they finally slowly turned the corner onto our property and parked, Topsy was unloaded from the horse trailer. The adults moved off, talking among themselves, leaving me holding his lead rope. Giddy and beaming, all I could think about was this had to be a dream; I was unable to believe he was really here.

To prove to myself this was all real, eagerly I leaned in to touch his face and buried my nose in his neck—inhaling deeply, lost in his unique horse scent of barn, hay, sweat, and even something sweet like honey. Looking into his big brown eyes that were looking back at me, unafraid and gentle, I began slowly moving around him to not startle or create any more stress for the little guy. Still stroking his face, then his back and each leg, I checked him carefully to make sure he was uninjured. Satisfied he was sound, instinctively, I wrapped my arms tightly around his neck, unwilling to release my hold, knowing he was home, and he was my pony.

That day, I fell in love for the first time.

I SPENT MY SUMMER DAYS often just playing outside with my sisters. When we were not playing together, my focus turned to reading, or I would wander off and be in my own world with nature and my pony.

Topsy wasn't much of a talker, so I spent a great deal of time with him in silence, wondering what he was thinking and why he would do certain things in a certain way. I often wandered off to sit quietly, watching newborn animals or simply sat in the sun, watching plants grow, wondering, *How does that work?*

I remember sitting perched on the kitchen porch step, watching the chickens move about our yard, wondering which came first, a chicken or an egg? I wondered who could I ask for that information? Little did I know, the chicken and the egg was an age-old question.

From those widely varied contemplations, my introspective thoughts evolved into many hours reflecting on things in my own head. That initiated some pretty amazing intuitive experiences.

It initially surprised me when I would ponder a question and an answer would pop into my head. How did I know that? And off my brain would go in that new direction, wondering what just happened.

Also naturally curious, Mother-Vic was introduced to Edgar Cayce books by a family member who was seeking solutions to several significant health conditions that stumped her doctors.

Mother-Vic was intrigued about this man and his legacy as an American clairvoyant—how he allegedly answered questions while asleep, on subjects as varied as healing, reincarnation, wars, Atlantis, and future events.

Bored one day, I plopped down in the easy chair and noticed the stack of these new books on the side table. Picking up the top book, I began reading, and everything I read was somehow making real sense. It felt as though my brain was a sponge for this information and my "self" was expanding the more I read.

In a matter of days, I finished reading all of them and noticed my dreams became more vivid. Many flying dreams so realistic, I was certain I could really fly. Often, I dreamt I was floating in the one corner of my bedroom, again certain this was real.

One improvement that made me very happy was when I faced Topsy and looked into his eyes; he appeared to look back at me with a knowing that created an even stronger connection between us.

These books also seemed to engage another level

of awareness for me—an awareness masquerading as another voice or perspective, words gently whispered into my ear or directly entering my thoughts. While sometimes startling, this also felt familiar, like an old friend offering suggestions that often saved my bacon.

ONE CAREFREE, SUMMER DAY, we kids were playing in the barnyard, climbing up and down the old, worn barn hayloft ladder from the ground to the upper level where the hay was stored. The ladder had been there since the ancient barn was built and was not the sturdiest structure.

We were running up and down that rickety ladder, then chasing each other around in the hayloft, racing to the ladder. I grabbed it to swing around to the steps and clamor down. Looking straight down the ladder chute, I suddenly noticed several old, discarded boards with large, dangerous, rusty nails exposed and sticking up.

Curious me scampered down the hayloft ladder to get a closer look. Feeling strongly compelled to hustle around and move those boards away from that floor area at the foot of the ladder, I stacked them against the far wall. In my head, I heard, "Just in case somebody loses their grip and falls."

My brain suddenly shifted to a very adult, responsible action taken by a nine-year-old kid, who, until that moment, was laser focused on running and playing. Even then, I thought to myself, *Where did THAT come from?*

Shrugging my shoulders at that weird shift in my

attention, another gentle mental nudge strongly convinced me to climb up the ladder and push a couple of bales of hay out of the loft and down to the floor. Tearing the bales apart, spreading the loose hay around that floor area, I was able to create somewhat of a cushion. Again, "Just in case somebody fell."

As the day wore on, it turned out it was me who fell out of the hayloft.

Carelessly playing, I lost my grip and fell twenty-plus feet from the top of the ladder, landing on my back into that somewhat safer, yet barely softer, location. Wow, that hurt.

After laying there a few seconds to gather myself after the surprise fall, I sat up to dust off the hay and finally pulled myself upright. I remember sitting there for a few more minutes because it was difficult to move, let alone stand up. When I finally did stand, my back was on fire. Standing straight was not an option.

Slowing walking around in an effort to loosen up and shake it off, it finally seemed to feel better, so we continued playing in the barn. Walking was painful but standing hunched over felt better than standing up so to get around that, I grabbed a bicycle and began riding it around the barnyard.

From the kitchen window, Mother-Vic caught a glimpse of me hunched over on the bicycle and called me over. She was drying her hands with a hand towel as she walked out the side porch door, "What's going on here?

Why are you walking funny and hunched over the bike handlebars?"

"Oh, I fell out of the barn and landed on my back." I said over my shoulder as I turned to pedal off.

She was not having that and banished me to the sofa as she called the doctor. Watching her on the phone calling a doctor was scarier than the fall. We could count on one hand the number of times any of us saw a doctor because calling a doctor wasn't something we did unless it was really serious. She made an immediate appointment with a local, blind chiropractor who, at that time, was the equivalent of a witch doctor.

Lying on his table while he made adjustments, I was thinking not only was it really weird that twisting me around on this table was supposed to make me feel better, but I also wondered why I felt motivated to stop playing long enough to create a small safety landing area at the foot of the ladder. I came to the conclusion that it was "just lucky."

The next day, I was back crawling around, and in a few short days, upright and again playing in the barn.

BACK IN THE LATE 1950'S, Mother-Vic and Dad would load us up in the family station wagon for short summer family vacations. We three girls excitedly settled into the back seat of the car as Dad enjoyed driving us down the winding, backwoods highways of the Midwest. Chattering and singing, we would gaze out the windows as he drove through the lush, green rolling countryside and down the bustling main streets of numerous small farm communities.

At that time, all the major roads passed through rural communities with thriving downtowns. The majority of these small, tidy communities' architectural focal points were their 1800s-era large stone municipal building surrounded by tall, mature, well-kept trees shading the walkways in the park-like settings of the town squares.

Before shopping malls, Walmarts, and truck stops, the communities supported their own small local businesses. Generations of family-owned department stores mimicked Sears, Roebuck, and Company or JC Penneys, the large retailers found only in more heavily populated communities.

Most communities boasted a full-service gas station, a locker for processing meat, a hardware store, a feed and grain store, several bars, often a drug or general store, and usually one or several neatly kept and well-attended local churches. And, in good weather, there was always an American flag proudly waving from the flagpole in front of the local post office and school.

In more active communities, there was at least one local café with veteran waitresses who knew everybody and greeted their regulars with a hearty, "Hey, Bobby. How ya doin'? How's the wife? The kids? Heard your son-in-law got himself a nice buck hunting with Jimmy last weekend. Here's your coffee. Say hey to Betty for me."

When the morning chores were completed, the local men would gather around the worn tables in the back of the café by the kitchen (quick access to a coffee refill) or in front, right next to the big picture window so they could watch the comings and goings around town.

Sitting at the same worn tables where their fathers and grandfathers met, drinking coffee, laughing, sharing tales, they, too, would greet the locals stopping by to gossip and learn the latest news. All the regulars would look over the tops of their coffee cups as they sipped, curious as they sized up folks stopping in who, like us, were "not from around here" and were just passing through.

Dad contentedly drove us from town to town, past crops, livestock, and neat, orderly Midwest farms scattered around the countryside as we robustly sang songs with Mother-Vic. She taught us harmonies, or we would sing rounds to the tunes of "Row, Row, Row Your Boat," "Lida Rose," or "Mr. Sandman." We would make up new games identifying unfamiliar license plates, spotting different animals in the distance or reading the Burma-Shave signs. How we all loved going on family road trips.

When we would slowly roll to a stop at an intersection, Dad would interrupt the songfest with a fun-loving shout, "Left or right?" We three girls would squeal over each other, "Left! Left! Right! Left! Right!" followed by a brief discussion. Once we reached a consensus, he would turn and point the car in the direction chosen. Off we would go to see what we might discover down this new road.

Along with the leisurely drive, another daily adventure was finding a stopping spot for the evening. Ideally, as we girls and the day wore down, I am certain my parents' fingers were crossed, hoping for luck that the next town would deliver an affordable hotel.

We could not believe our good fortune when, in the small town of Chillicothe, Missouri, we located a motel with a swimming pool, and we were there in enough time to spend most of the rest of the day in the pool. We were the only people in the pool, and we took full advantage of all that water.

Holding our noses, we jumped into the shallow end, scampered to the pool ladder on the side of the pool, and did it again. Dad picked us up and threw us high in the air, and we'd splash down, coming back to him with, "Do it again!" We were all disappointed to leave the following morning. However, that brief letdown would soon be forgotten as we began singing and looking forward to what this day might bring because Mother-Vic instilled in us when we were disappointed that "there is always tomorrow." She was a firm believer in the great promise of a different perspective and renewed optimism brought forth in "the light of a new day."

More than once, we found a small town with a motel later in the day than Mother-Vic would have liked. Some days, we passed motel opportunities simply because the road looked inviting, so why stop? Or the alternative was we stopped earlier because we all felt like it.

On those days when we ran out of daylight, Mother-Vic, bouncing down the road in the front seat next to Dad, would retrieve a map and flashlight from the glove box and balance both as she studied the situation to determine our location and the next town. To us, it almost felt like she was "cheating", but as a parent, for Mother-Vic to resort to the map was likely a choice between promptly finding a town/motel or strangling us.

WHEN I WAS IN THE THIRD or fourth grade, our summer Bible school teacher asked us to share how we spent our summer vacation. One classmate offered their family was traveling to St. Louis to visit the zoo.

Slowly turning in my seat to look at him, staring, I was dumbfounded and feeling a little bit sorry for him. Musing, *Wow. That's so sad. You already know where you are going? Where's the fun in that?*

Those little jaunts provided significant lessons in communication, teamwork when picking a direction, the ability to go with the flow, how to be OK with being open to whatever happens, and most importantly, they instilled confidence that we would figure out what we needed to do, no matter what challenges these adventures provided.

Later in life, I experienced my own personal "aha moments" as I naturally applied these lessons. A good example was when I fully grasped that in my life journey, there was no right or wrong way to reach my personal destination. Rather, would I choose the long way or the short way? Either way, why not enjoy the ride because I will reach a destination, even if it wasn't where I thought I was going.

Those lessons easily translated to the many magical hours I spent with Topsy. Anytime the weather allowed me outside, it typically meant spending some part of my day with Topsy. It may have been me just lazing around in the pasture with him, oftentimes simply laying on his back as he slowly moved around the field, grazing.

I loved the feel of the sun on my face, his rhythmic chewing, and feeling his entire body slowly move as he leisurely picked up one hoof at a time to step to another spot of fresh grass, grazing and letting his tail lazily flick to swish away the noisy, buzzing flies. Occasionally, his tail flicking became a bit more aggressive and whisks of his tail brushed across my cheek, which not only stung but often made me giggle.

After a while, he might be ready to find a cool, shady spot out of the direct sunlight, or he might have moseyed to a different location. Pulling myself up, stretching my arms, my back and legs, and with my knees, I would gently urge Topsy to meander through fields to explore the small pasture creek. Jumping off him to open the pasture gate, I would guide him out of the confines of his enclosure to roam freely. It would simply be Topsy as he wandered with me, a small human attachment on his bare back, wondering what he was thinking and where he would take us today.

Once we ventured out, we were often out all day. Usually around lunchtime, my rumbling stomach motivated me to search out a handful of fresh wild berries, strawberries, or a fresh green apple from one of the many apple trees growing wild in the area.

Sliding off Topsy's back, I might rustle around in the garden to find a fresh, juicy, ripe tomato. Topsy would start grazing as I plopped down into the tall grass, or under a shady tree, or near the creek with my feet dangling in the cool, gently flowing water. Stretching out, I reached into my shorts pocket to retrieve that small shaker of salt that I had hastily shoved in there as I ran out the door several hours earlier.

I sat quietly, enjoying each bite into that tomato as I ate it like an apple, listening to the nature sounds and observing Topsy—just watching the day go by. Was it any wonder I would fiddle away the day and lose track of time?

When we finally wandered home at day's end, sauntering into the kitchen, I greeted Mother-Vic. Plopping down into an ancient aluminum kitchen chair to talk with her as she prepared dinner, we discussed Topsy and my adventure of the day.

While it did not happen often, there were times she shared her concern that perhaps I had been gone too long and returned too late in the day. No matter how many times she mentioned that, it just never stuck with me as an issue because when I was with Topsy, I felt safe and time was inconsequential.

Even as adults, we three girls often checked in with each other and Mother-Vic. When she was satisfied "all her little chickadees" were home safe, especially after dark or in bad weather, only then did she tell us she could relax.

GROWING RAPIDLY, it was when I was about twelve years old that we started looking for a larger pony.

Dad and Mother-Vic purchased Pepper from a local family. Pepper was a barely broken part-quarter horse and part-Morgan. When I got on him, he reared up and tried very hard to toss me. Startled, I hung on and thought it was the greatest thing to go from comfortable, sweet, gentle Topsy to having that much horse under me.

It took some talking before I finally convinced Dad and Mother-Vic that Pepper was the right horse for me. They made the transaction, and then big surprise, he would not load into the horse trailer. My only other option was to hook a lead to his halter and walk him the five miles of gravel road to our house.

From there, I just hung out with him and Topsy as they became acquainted. Not having any horse training or anybody to ask about how to handle this green broke horse, I simply formulated my own plan.

Over the remainder of the summer, I figured out how to get him to accept a bridle and bit by placing a sugar cube in my hand and offering to him. He loved that. So, I thought, *Hey, if I lay the cube in my hand and lay the bit over it, he'll eat the cube, and at the right time, I can slip the bit into his mouth.* That worked, so I eventually was able to slide the bridle over his head and like a dog, talk to him and walk him all over the property and roads, often placing my arm across his neck, then his back, until he eventually accepted a saddle blanket on his back during our long walks.

When the day finally came to try to ride him, I led him over to the wood fence and clamored up it to get high enough to slowly lower myself onto his back. He was unsure what to do with that extra weight and was lightly bucking and very skittish at first—not as skittish as Mother-Vic when she saw me come around the property riding on his back. In retrospect, I realize I could've been badly hurt, and Mother-Vic may have found me lying in the pasture had this stage not gone well.

I continued familiarizing him with me, and then the extra weight and mechanics of a saddle, until he was fully able to ride for fun and to show in the local summer horse shows.

OUR SMALL FARM COMMUNITY thrived on the "work hard, play hard" ethic, which is typical within rural culture. As soon as kids are old enough to learn and participate in the chores, they are shadowing the adults in order to learn the ropes. From feeding and watering the farm dogs and cats, to watching equipment repairs, to listening while adults discussed farm business, we pitched in when we could. Families and neighbors worked hard together, celebrating and supporting personal and community accomplishments.

Most of our community knew each other and their extended families. Many parents and grandparents grew up together, married, and started families, making most local celebrations more like a very large family reunion.

High school graduation in a small town is one of the highlights of the end of that school year. Kids make their plans for college, a trade school, military, or working the family farm or business. Many married right out of high school. Nearly everybody had their future plans lined up.

Except me.

My life to this point was by the books—parents, family, school, church, and follow the rules. Plus, as I became more involved in school activities and a more active social and dating scene, my parents sold Pepper and donated Topsy to a neighboring family with two small children. This family was in no position to purchase a pony, and we knew they would take great care of him. When the day they came for Topsy to leave us, those two kids were beside themselves. As much as it broke my heart to be handing him to another family, because of all my other activities, it had been quite some time since I had ridden or spent time with Pepper or Topsy, and these were the best situations for all of us.

With graduation on the horizon, I saw new options! Those opportunities triggered the wanderlust, adventurer gene that I only suspected I carried, yet never fully applied. With graduation, an entire new world of possibilities opened up, and in my soul, I knew I would soon leave the security of my safe, happy, and fun home.

1944. Mildred LaVonne "Vicki" McVicker as a young college student. Age 20, Coe College, Cedar Rapids, Iowa

1948. Phillip James "Phil" Peterson. Age 23 with his beloved Harley in a small town in Iowa. Notice the enormous pile of discarded corn cobs on the right side of the photo.

May, 1951. Dad seated on the sofa at home in Eagle Grove, Iowa—holding me for the first time.

Summer, 1950's. Preparing for a road trip and the folks would set us in the luggage rack as a "treat," but it was really to keep us out of their hair while they packed up our Ford station wagon.

1950's. Shari in a boat with Dad on some Midwestern lake, taking stock of this fishing excursion.

1950's. Mother-Vic looking over her chickadees: Shari, Marilyn, and Margaret/Madge.

Late 1950's. Margaret/Madge, Dad, Shari, Mother-Vic and Marilyn at home. We girls were so proud of our matching pajamas we received for Christmas.

Early 1960's. Shari and Topsy, wearing a hat I made for him, at our Toddville property. Behind us is Dad's woodpile and the boards that served as our sidewalk when it was muddy, leading to the back porch steps and into the kitchen.

Early 1960's. On the Toddville property, Shari on Topsy pulling a cart Dad made. It had steel wheels and the ride was so bumpy, but it never stopped us from loading up the neighbor kids and Marilyn (on the far right) for a ride.

Early 1960's. Shari with Pepper and Margaret/Madge with Topsy, standing in the front yard of our Toddville acreage with the horse pasture behind us.

Early 1960's. Easter morning with Dad, Mother-Vic, Margaret/Madge, Marilyn, and Shari. Behind us is the creaky front porch of our Toddville house.

Chapter Three

UNCLE BUD WAS A MAN of few words; he was a man of action. He was not only a farmer, crop duster, and multitalented musician, he was a bit of a character who fully embraced his belief that adventures were the best way to learn about life.

Here's an example: Uncle Bud's days often found him driving into town to run an errand. One day, when filling his truck at the local gas station, he struck up a conversation with a stranger who also happened to be filling the gas tank of a new motorhome. The stranger was transporting this vehicle across country and suggested perhaps Uncle Bud would like to ride along and help drive.

At the hint of a suggestion of a spontaneous experience, Uncle Bud simply parked his truck, climbed on board the motorhome, and let the escapade begin!

Hours later, at their next stop, Uncle Bud located a pay phone to call his wife, Aunt Gladys. As direct as he was, the conversation likely went this direction, "I'm in Rapid City, transporting a motorhome to Seattle. I'll call you from the Des Moines airport when I return." And with that, off he went.

At the drop of a hat, Uncle Bud, often with Aunt Gladys, was game to head out on one of their many ventures. Something as simple as going into town to leave some freshly baked goods at the church for the bake sale might present an opportunity for fun. They would come home two weeks later to find the lunch they were planning to eat "when they returned from town" was still sitting out on the kitchen counter.

Aunt Gladys could only shake her head, giggle at her handsome, kind husband, and go along with Uncle Bud's crazy antics. She kept a small bag by the back door, packed with a change of clothes for both of them. She never knew when she might grab that bag as they headed out, should her instincts alert her today could be an adventure day, "Just in case." When our extended family gathered together, Uncle Bud would show up and head over to mingle among the adults, seldom talking, mostly listening. When he was done with the small talk and getting antsy for some action, he would wander over to his vehicle and pull out his drum set, his saxophone, a keyboard, or any of his collection of instruments to organize a jam session featuring the young cousins.

Other times at their farm, he might ramble over to simply hang out among the group of kid cousins, and we adored hanging out with him. He would sit and talk with us, asking questions about our lives and what we were doing. Or as he milled around playing with the kids, he would lean back in a cowboy/farmer manner, put his work gnarled hands in his pockets, gaze up at the sky, and muse to himself, yet loudly enough to tempt us "Looks like a good day to fly" or a more direct "Let's go up."

The air would fill with squeals and claps as we scampered after him to see who would be first selected to crawl with him into one of his single engine airplanes.

To ensure a fun ride, he would take the small plane and passengers up, buzzing over the Iowa fields, executing gentle loops and turns and giving the kids some time on the controls. Our elders naturally coached us, even when doing the smallest of tasks. For Uncle Bud, his favorite subject was the basics of flight.

He triggered a sense of pending adventure when the giant doors on his small, outbuilding hanger slid open, and he would manually pull the airplane into the sun.

After executing his pre-check and starting the engine, he would slowly taxi to the end of the farm runway. Double checking the controls and gauges, he would turn the small aircraft to launch.

My heart would pound as I held on to the dashboard in front of me, straining to peek up and over it at the magical, open runway that stretched before us.

Revving the engine, the aircraft would begin moving forward. Gradually picking up speed as it raced over the uneven, bumpy grass airstrip, I felt the sudden and incredible freeing of the nose lifting and the ground falling away. Leaving the runway, we drifted upwards, rising above the trees.

Then airborne, he made a hard turn, for no reason other than it was great fun. Higher and higher we climbed, swooping, swirling, simply riding the wind. I closed my eyes, enjoying the ride, wishing this flight would never end.

Little did I know that spending time with that beloved character in the cockpits of his small planes during such a young age would play such a significant role in my mental state during and after United 811.

WE WERE VISITING Uncle Bud and Aunt Glady's farm one summer day when, in his usual fashion, he decided it was a good day to "go up."

Hearing that was music to my ears! I raced to the hangar to "help" him pull one of his aircrafts into the bright sunlight, impatiently squirming, following him, asking questions during his preparation and pre-check. Gassing it up and checking it out, he set the brakes and chocked the wheels. Satisfied, he easily lifted me off the ground, laughing as he swung me into the seat, then reached across to buckle me in and gave it a good solid tug, checking it twice.

Assured all was in place, he jumped into his seat, and with a big grin on his face, turned the aircraft toward the freshly mowed runway. He revved the engine, and off we went.

Weaving and sashaying in the beautiful, blue, calm summer sky, we enjoyed the magnificent view, flying low over the fields, checking crops, soaring higher for altitude in order to swoop down to buzz over his livestock.

Suddenly, this new multidimensional aspect of flight dawned on me. My brain went to *Hey, wait a minute— we are not moving in the familiar, four grounded movements of forward, backward, left, and right when we are up here. We also get to move up and down.* That realization captivated my imagination and suddenly made perfect sense. Even at such a young age, this revelation, in some way, unlocked my curiosity about other possibilities.

As a child, of course, I had only experienced the four familiar movements, believing they were the only way people could move about. Having recognized these new up/down options, Uncle Bud tasked me with keeping an eye out for air traffic and anything unusual. All this revelation in a few minutes simply blew my small child's mind.

Flying on this day, we were moving around in, what to me, was another dimension. I pondered this as we flew over the neatly kept farms and the small towns that dotted the landscape with their connecting roads. In awe, I gazed down at the vastness and possibilities of roads stretching as far as the eye could see, the impossibly straight rows of corn, the meandering creeks, large, leafy trees scattered along the banks, deep paths worn into the landscape from generations of livestock plodding nose to tail between the pastures and back to the barn at dusk. Nearly giddy, I felt as though I had just been let in on some big cosmic secret.

Marveling at the rich colors and natural beauty of the Iowa farmland below, I was content, relishing the mysteries and freedom of flight. Then, without a word, Uncle Bud leaned over, twisted the single ignition key, and it was suddenly silent—the engine stopped.

As unexpected, and dare I say, crazy, as that was, when I looked over at him, my first thought was, *I wonder what this is about?* trusting him implicitly in what I was certain was going to be another great Uncle Bud adventure.

In this completely unexpected new experience, he calmly looked over at me, even though we were flying with no engine noise, and said, "Enjoy the view, but always be alert and look for an alternate landing strip. Even with a flight plan, you never know when you will need an alternate safe place to land. Trust yourself; have good and working equipment plus a backup plan."

With that advice, he asked me to spot landing options

by searching immediate locations as well as distant possibilities. Peering out over the landscape, I looked at what was a few moments ago simply a beautiful view. I now needed to assess this view with a different eye—as a "backup plan."

All around us were open fields and relatively flat gravel roads. There were countless options, and I was fully believing that heck, this was a piece of cake to set this plane down anywhere. Because I could see and accept we had options, I felt giddy and happy that even with no engine, we would be OK.

He, too, was looking around, pointing and teaching why any possible location may or may not be a good possibility. Maybe the field was too short and landing there would run us into trees, or landing there was too close to dangerous power lines, or curvy roads would create an unsafe obstacle.

He was smiling and clearly tickled to see I was taking all this in stride. Turning, he nodded his head, which I interpreted to mean he had selected one of the alternative landing choices in our immediate sight. Rather, he reached over and turned the key, and the engine jumped back to life.

We returned to our lazy loops and turns until we turned and headed for home.

Early 1960's. Uncle Bud, Aunt Gladys, and Maryann, their only child. Maryann struggled with significant medical challenges her entire life and passed away at age 23 due to complications.

Chapter Four

A FEW MONTHS PRIOR to my high school graduation, Uncle Bud approached me with an offer. Would I
consider moving to their Terril home, in northwest Iowa,
where he would train me as a crop duster, or as referred
to today, an ag pilot?

In the 1960's, the image of a crop duster was of a
man flying a small plane over fields in rural settings. The
plane swooped down over the field, then laid down a fine
mist of fertilizer or insect repellant spray, pulling up just
before flying into the power lines and disappearing, only
to come around to spray the next set of crop rows.

The flying is technically challenging, occasionally

hazardous, sometimes bordering on dare devil. The pilot must be precise and alert to avoid trees, powerlines, livestock, and structural hazards, to name a few. Pilots must know what they are doing, not only in the air but with all aspects of aerial application, insects, and safe pesticide usage.

After the proposed training, and when he felt confident I could handle his crop-dusting enterprise, an arrangement would be on the table for me to take over his reputable business and farm. He was looking to retire, and this was an incredible, generous offer.

He shared the big picture with me: the financial aspects, the work, the responsibilities, and also the long days and long hours during the growing season of May through September. When experiencing good weather, a typical day would consist of rising before dawn to prepare the plane and supplies for dusting crops in the still, early morning hours and then dusting again in the calm early evening dusk.

The hours between peak dusting times would be busy working around the farm, tending to livestock should I choose to raise them, maintaining the aircraft, reloading the chemicals, and securing customers, all things necessary to run the farm and the business. He reminded me there would likely be little social interaction in this remotely located 24-7 business.

In the winters, things could be pretty much whatever I desired. Perhaps, I could remain in northwest Iowa to immerse myself in the community—or travel, or maybe winter in a warmer climate, or even fly to another part of the country to work dousing wildfires for firefighting crews, survey land, fly banners over sporting events, or whatever additional flying jobs became available.

His offer was appealing—after flying with him, it was apparent I was a frustrated pilot. The income potential was generous, plus their farm property was beautiful.

My thoughts were torn between the flying opportunity countered by, why would I leave my small 390-person community and move 250 miles to a more remote and even smaller community in northwest Iowa?

Had I accepted the offer, I would have likely enjoyed every minute, but I simply could not see it then.

This was my first adult "standing at the crossroad" decision—those decisions that set a course in our lives that may define us. I knew this wasn't the right opportunity at this time.

ANOTHER GENEROUS postgraduation opportunity was a full scholarship to play basketball and run track for John F. Kennedy College, a small liberal arts school located in eastern Nebraska.

Now defunct, JFK was one of the first and few colleges to offer athletic scholarship opportunities for women in the 1960's.

During my senior year in high school, a full scholarship based on athletics was a great opportunity for a woman. My high school basketball coach and I drove to Nebraska and toured the campus. We met the coaching staff; then I worked out with their basketball team. Shortly after the visit, a letter arrived from JFK. Nervously opening the envelope, I was ecstatic to see it contained the scholarship offer we discussed. At this point, I was fully on board to accept it.

The calendar marched from the cold, dark winter months to sunny spring, and my high school graduation loomed on the horizon. Now feeling less certain about the four-year JFK commitment, I realized that once I graduated, there was another big, unknown world out there to explore. Plus, my restless, wanderlust was kicking in, and I was torn.

MAY, 1969. High school graduation wishes and cards were pouring in, including one from my Iowa cousin Pat who was a recent transplant to Honolulu.

Rather than the pattern of college or marriage after high school, Pat had chosen to live in Honolulu, "Mary Tyler Moore style," as a young, single, professional woman living on her own. I was intrigued with her lifestyle as that option was nowhere on my here-is-my-future radar in 1969.

I tore open the envelope containing her card that accompanied her graduation gift, and found she had included a short, chatty letter. She offered her best wishes and then mentioned her Hawaii roommate was getting married and relocating from Honolulu back to the mainland, ending her note with, "If you ever think about moving to Hawaii after graduation, I'm looking for a roommate."

You know when someone says something that smacks you right in the chest and *oomph*, there's no turning back? It took me all of about two seconds to realize—that's IT! *Moving to Hawaii is exactly what I am going to do.*

Nearly giddy with anticipation and determined this was the best choice for me, I pulled Mother-Vic and Dad to the kitchen table, barely able to contain my eagerness to share this decision.

My presentation was short: "The idea of college or moving to northwest Iowa is not nearly as appealing as moving to Honolulu. Pat will be my roommate. She is responsible with a good job, slightly older than me, and familiar with the area and life there. Plus, Pat is a close relative you know well and fully trust."

Silence—they looked at each other, back at me, and without hesitation, both shook their heads in the affirmative, which signaled to me their total, unconditional support.

It was dizzying how quickly this all was happening, and my parents had a few questions. Was I ready to accept the consequences of foregoing taking over a thriving business or walking away from a full college scholarship for Hawaii? What was my plan for money to even travel to Hawaii?

I gave confident, "Yup, I'll figure it out," answers to all their questions. Then smiling, my Dad offered, "OK, but no talking to sailors, and don't go out at night." Um, OK. Sure thing, Dad.

With all the excitement, it was suddenly June, 1969. A mere three weeks after I gave our high school commencement speech at graduation, and having just turned eighteen years old, I found myself winging my way to Hawaii on United Airlines.

Chapter Five

MOVING TO HONOLULU
1969

LITTLE DID I REALIZE that by leaving the rural community routines, safety, security, and coziness of Alburnett, there was a big life lesson surprise waiting for me. Ready for it? My surprise, or even aha moment, was that the Alburnett lifestyle, ethics, and code of conduct were not necessarily the model under which the rest of the world operated.

So, how did I get from Alburnett, Iowa, to Honolulu in June, 1969? After making the decision and realizing this was really going to happen, I sat down and counted the money I received as high school graduation gifts, and it totaled $126. Along with this cash from well wishes, my parents generously gifted me a silver, dainty, grown-up wristwatch, plus a set of matched luggage to signify their blessing of my decision.

Since spring, high school friends had been busy planning out their graduation and life beyond high school. Several were looking forward to college, a few were getting married shortly after graduation, and many were already busy working with their families on their farms. While I was excited and happy for my friends and their plans, my focus shifted to Hawaii.

The excitement and anticipation of my great adventure became my first thoughts in the morning and last thoughts at night. There was no hesitation as I began packing the few clothing and personal items I was taking and tucking away the rest that I was leaving behind.

In June 1969, United Airlines offered a significant student-discounted standby fare. After purchasing their $100 one-way ticket from Cedar Rapids to Honolulu, via Chicago and Los Angeles, I took a deep breath and fanned out the few remaining bills on the kitchen table. There was twenty-six dollars, the grand total of my remaining funds.

Only two years earlier, I had experienced my first commercial airline flight as a high school sophomore, traveling solo nonstop from Cedar Rapids to Oklahoma City to attend a week-long basketball camp. My first experience was a simple process to check in, check my bag, board, fly, land, and retrieve my bag. Go to camp, then repeat the flight process for the return home. Easy peasy.

This Honolulu flight, my second commercial flight ever, involved connecting flights. As a travel novice, I was completely unaware bags could be checked through to the final destination.

On the morning of my departure, checking my two new graduation gift suitcases to Chicago, I excitedly departed Cedar Rapids, Iowa. Upon arrival in Chicago, I picked them up at baggage claim and took a walk to check them in for the next flight to Los Angeles.

Upon arrival in Los Angeles, I again picked up the bags in baggage claim, then walked back to the counter to recheck them for the flight to Honolulu. On the way, I dropped the smaller of the two bags, and my contents spilled all over the floor of the busy Los Angeles terminal.

As a young woman, I was horrified to see my undergarments scattered in the open. Several kind people immediately stopped to help. Panicked, I shoveled everything back into the suitcase, and then, flustered, struggled to close it. Managing that, I scurried off completely humiliated, wondering why I hadn't even thought to lock the suitcases.

Looking back, I often wondered why the ticket agents at each airport, seeing my ticket itinerary as they obviously checked then rechecked my bag, didn't ask any questions or say something to me about checking the bags through. That I retrieved and then rechecked bags at each stop made perfect sense to me as standard operating procedure based on my extensive (not) airline travel experience, along with my don't-expect-anybody-to-take-care-of-you advice from Dad.

Outside of the dropped suitcase, this exercise also became an opportunity for me to explore different airports. It seemed sensible that it was my responsibility to ensure my bags followed me on each flight, but I thought it would be nice if the airlines made this process a little easier.

What did surprise me—and I still shake my head at it today—is that once I settled in for the final leg out of Los Angeles to Honolulu, I imagined my journey was nearly complete. Looking out the window and halfway listening to the flight crew go through their announcements including flight time information, I nearly shot out of my seat when they announced the approximately five-hour flight time from Los Angeles to Honolulu.

How naïve of me to imagine this would be a short flight, maybe thirty to forty-five minutes. Honolulu is just off the coast of California, right? What? Nearly five hours flight time? Where the heck *is* Hawaii?

I immediately removed the route map from the seat pocket in front of me to search for Hawaii. Squinting, I searched for the Hawaiian Islands off the coast of California—near maybe Catalina. Then I noticed the familiar outline of Hawaii's tiny islands way out there in the middle of the ocean. Looking up from the map, I gulped

THE VIEW FROM 13F

and wondered if the flight crew could even find Hawaii. This was the first time my thoughts regarding my journey were, *Uh, oh—what AM I doing!*

Since I was already settled into my window seat, I figured I may as well sit back and ride it out. The large jet lifted off from Los Angeles and circled over the city to gain speed and altitude as we began the long Pacific crossing.

Los Angeles, the mainland, and Iowa faded out of view from my window, disappearing into the distance—realistically and symbolically. No worries; this was going to be an even greater adventure than I had imagined!

Once we reached cruising altitude, winging our way west, *far* west, the two fidgety gals seated to my left were finally settled in for the long flight.

Taking stock of my seatmates, I was intrigued so see they were two poster girls for the 1960's hip Southern California life and were clearly friends. Young, fit, tan, each wearing their long, sun-bleached hair parted down the middle, they smelled faintly of patchouli and what I later discovered was weed. They both wore low riding, long, colorful paisley skirts, flamboyant embroidered tops, headbands, rings, bracelets, and necklaces—all the trinkets and bangles of the "far out" California '60s.

Saying hello, I introduced myself and learned they were Celeste and Harmony—two childhood friends who were moving from Los Angeles to Maui to embark on their own great adventure.

We immediately discovered the common ground of recently graduating high school, and then the conversation turned to why we were all moving to Hawaii. As hip Southern California city girls, they were simply seeking a new scene, and 1969 Hawaii was certainly the place to be.

They were as curious about me, as they had never met someone from a small, Midwestern, farming community. Introductions and preliminary conversations aside, they began asking many questions about my life in rural America, and I could see my simple and happy family and life basically amazed them—telephone party lines, unpaved streets, school, church, and family made up 95 percent of our social life—football in the fall, planting in the spring, long, lazy summers. No ocean, no freeways, no traffic, no crime, no cities with theatre, no celebrities, no pro sports or fine dining. No beaches and certainly no eternal sunshine.

When they described their life, I pondered their "normal," which was picking out the brand-new muscle cars they were gifted at age sixteen, pool parties, drinking, drugs, designer clothes, "who they knew," and the incredible freedoms they shared as their parents were seldom home, busy with their own lives. With little involvement in their kid's choices, it became clear their parents were basically strangers and a bother to them. Listening, incredulous, I realized these two friends, with little or no parental guidance, basically raised themselves together.

Just wow.

That city mouse/country mouse disparity became even more apparent as we finally approached Honolulu. Early in our conversation, I shared my initial surprise at the distance Hawaii was from the mainland. At that, the sideway glances between the two of them were clearly, "Oh, brother!"

However, that story was about to be topped.

We had been seated together nearly five hours where we enjoyed nonstop chatter about our lives. When the captain interrupted to announce our final approach to Honolulu, the flight crew began to prepare the cabin for landing by picking up trash, checking tray tables and seats, and other normal flight duties. There was a lull in our conversation as we realized when we landed, our journeys would take us in other directions, and we wondered what was next for all of us.

Leaning against the window, lost in my thoughts, I watched as the distant island and the unmistakable silhouette of Diamond Head came into view. My eyes searched for the long stretches of empty white sandy beaches and beach shacks with thatched roofs and tropical foliage I had envisioned.

Instead, there were lights. What were these endless lights that went as far as I could see? Turning to Harmony, I asked, "Um, what's with all the lights?"

She leaned over to look out the window past me, "Oh, that's just the city."

Sputtering, I blurted out my first thought, "City! Honolulu is a CITY!" Who knew?

When we landed, Celeste and Harmony realized, "Bummer, dude" they missed their connecting flight to Maui. Without hesitation, I suggested they come along with me, certain Pat would be agreeable to return them for their six a.m. morning departure—plus, it seemed like the neighborly thing to do.

In 1969, a person did not just pick up the phone and make a long-distance call, unless someone died. It had to be a significant event because a long-distance call charge could be as much as three to five dollars each. Organizing this Hawaiian adventure with Pat was accomplished via handwritten letters back and forth in the US mail. My final letter shared my planned departure date, and because I was flying student standby and could be bumped to another flight, that I would call her upon landing.

Locating the nearest payphone in the Honolulu airport, I nervously dialed Pat. There was no answer, and there were no answering machines at that time.

Hanging up, I stood there, pondering what to do. My only contacts for Pat were her home phone and via US mail. Carrying Pat's last letter with her contact info as I contemplated options, my gaze drifted over toward some enthusiastic chatter and laughter.

A couple of local boys were standing near the curb, seemingly just hanging out, so I wandered over to show them the address and asked, "Do you guys know where this is?" Their immediate response was, "No *pilikia*! We drive you." (Translated from Hawaiian Pidgin: "No problem. We'll drive you there.")

Stacking our minimal luggage into the trunk, Celeste, Harmony, and I piled into the back seat of their car, and off we went. This was my first Hawaiian experience, and it was not a supreme act of confidence. It was simply what I would do had I been home.

We arrived at the address and parked in front of a neatly kept, four-story apartment building. Our two new Hawaiian friends chattered and laughed as they unloaded our belongings onto the curb. With a hearty wave of the *shaka* sign (the Hawaiian hand signal representing the "aloha spirit" feeling of friendship, gratitude, or solidarity) and shouts of best wishes for our move to their Aloha State, we watched their taillights disappear down the street and into the night. Then, standing in silence, we looked around to assess our situation.

We were three weary, young travelers with a ragtag assortment of luggage and backpacks at our feet, standing alone on a quiet residential street somewhere in Honolulu.

While getting our bearings, we heard some movement and looked up toward the sound of the soft chatter. Shadows of Pat and Sandy, a longtime friend of Pat's, were walking across the third-floor outdoor hallway toward Pat's apartment. They were clearly engrossed in their conversation, laughing as they relived their dinner and show with legendary Hawaiian entertainer and

Hawaii's "favorite son" Don Ho. He was well-known for his version of "Tiny Bubbles" and was a local celebrity who entertained people with Hawaiian music for five decades. What better way to celebrate Sandy's last night in town before returning to Iowa in the morning?

"HEEYYY!" I shouted, sounding very much like Gomer Pyle. That shout startled Pat, and she nearly jumped out of her skin, as she was not expecting anybody to be lurking in the street near her building.

Once she recognized us, she burst out laughing and motioned us to come on up. Grabbing our stuff off the curb, we clamored up the three flights of stairs to greet them. Pat, Sandy, Celeste, Harmony, and I were all simultaneously introducing ourselves and talking over each other, which created even more babble as we entered her home.

In the midst of all this commotion, I offered Pat a brief explanation of why I had two seeming drifters with me. She scurried around and eventually settled Sandy, the two strangers, and me around the floor, sofa, and floor cushions of this tiny, 426-square-foot studio apartment.

Everyone finally quieted down as we unwound into our own little slice of space we carved out in the small area. It was then that I mentioned my offer of Pat driving Celeste and Harmony to the airport for their six a.m. flight. Pat's reply? "No *pilikia*!"

AFTER ALL THE EXCITEMENT of the night, the morning arrived a few short hours later. Everybody finished hustling around the small apartment, gathering their belongings, and we all loaded into Pat's car for the early morning seven-mile drive to the airport.

We first dropped the California girls off for their Maui flight, then more goodbyes as we dropped Sandy for her flight to the mainland. After the excited and sad goodbyes for both departures, Pat and I returned to her apartment and my new home.

We talked briefly before she had to go. I watched as she pulled the apartment door closed and raced to catch the bus to her legal secretary job in downtown Honolulu. The lock clicked behind her, and it was then just me, standing alone in the middle of a strangely silent and very new environment.

In the still and quiet, I noticed the gentle, warm morning tropical breeze that passed through the louvres of the slightly opened jalousie windows lining the outside wall. Through the open louvres, I caught a glimpse of an unusual looking tree. Curiosity moved me closer to the windows, and I inhaled the sweet, citrusy smell floating in the breeze—a light, tropical scent like nothing I'd ever smelled before. Could that enchanting aroma have come from the tree?

I chuckled to myself as I compared the odd-looking tree outside the window to the sturdy maple and oak trees of Iowa that didn't look or smell like that. I watched, mesmerized, as the breeze gently moved the light-colored petals.

That was my introduction to the popular plumeria tree—this beautiful tree, right outside our window, was where many handmade flower leis were created for friends, visitors, and family.

I stood at the window, soaking up the soft breeze and deeply inhaling the sweet scent of the tree; the morning breeze was coming alive with layers of aromas of different and unique breakfast foods being prepared all around me.

New sounds of tropical birds chimed in, and there were enormous, fluffy white clouds against the backdrop of the most brilliant blue skies I had ever seen. Completing the scene was bright sunshine all around.

Fascinated, I marveled how, in just a matter of hours, many changes had occurred to my thinking, my living arrangements, and then my environment. The day before, I did not know any of this existed. Yet, that day, I stood smack in the middle of it all.

AFTER A FEW MINUTES, I came to attention, breaking the spell. Shaking my head to see if this was all a dream, I reminded myself of my responsibilities and reluctantly stepped away from the window.

The first item on my agenda was writing my family to advise them I had arrived safely and all was well.

Seeing a beautiful Hawaiian scene postcard on the kitchen counter, I penned a quick note, grabbed Pat's car keys, and scurried down the three flights of stairs to the ground floor garage. Locating Pat's red 1960 Ford Sunliner convertible, I jumped in and headed out for the short drive to the post office.

Most of my life had been spent in small communities, and just hours ago, my home was a town of less than 400 people. In my world, when Pat pointed down the street indicating the post office was "that way." How far away could it be?

Although the post office was maybe five to seven blocks "that way," as I began to drive , the next thing I knew, my sense of direction had checked out. I was clearly distracted with the convertible top down, sunny, warm breezes and the swaying palm trees all around as I motored along, my left arm hanging over the driver side door. Snapping out of my daydream, I realized, *Hey, these people are driving really fast. Whoa ... where am I?*

Looking around, I realized I was driving on the freeway for the first time, and I felt no concern. This was the first morning of the first day of my new Hawaiian adventure and my first time stepping out of the apartment. Suddenly, I was lost on a freeway, giddy as an even greater sense of adventure kicked in. After all, where's the panic—I reminded myself it was an island and unless I drive off the island, how lost could I get?

Not knowing or recognizing any landmarks, streets, or cross streets and not knowing exactly where I lived or if there was even a map in the car, somehow my internal autopilot instincts kicked in.

Looking ahead, it seemed getting off this busy free-way at the next exit was a good idea. Dodging speed-ing cars, I wove toward a quick right onto the next exit. Having never driven on an interstate, I thought this fast and frenetic freeway driving was really cool.

By then on unfamiliar back streets, turning on in-stinct, I reminded myself I had not driven that far on the interstate. Somehow, I found my way back to the apart-ment building.

This was before GPS and cell phones, so no one was more surprised than me to see Citron Street, the street where I then lived, or that I'd recognized the apartment building I saw for the first time only once last night in the dark and again in my rearview mirror as I left that morning.

Pulling into the parking area, I noticed an outgo-ing mail slot near the bank of mailboxes (something I had never seen before) and simply dropped the post-card in there.

Sharing the story with Pat that evening, she was sur-prised at the circumstances that somehow landed me back at my new home. I realized years later how improb-able it was that I made it back that easily—clearly an-other case of trusting my instincts and staying calm, as someone had to be watching over me even then.

The following two years were a blur of new experi-ences, starting with my first weekend on Oahu. To show me the sights, Pat loaded the car with beach mats, tow-els, sunscreen, and snacks as we headed toward the other side of the island for my first ever beach experience.

Having little frame of reference for what we were about to experience, other than TV, magazines, and photographs, I was beyond excited as we pulled into the beach area parking lot. There were no words for the postcard-perfect view that lay out in front of me.

Gasping and yanking on the door handle, I looked upon my first sight of the endless blue water. The door flew open as I tumbled out of the passenger seat onto the parking lot pavement like a clumsy ten-week-old puppy, bounding, jumping, squealing, blubbering, and pointing toward the mystical and rhythmic sound of the surf as it crashed all around me. Racing to the ocean's edge, I stood in awe as the water splashed over my feet and receded back into the ocean.

My heart soared in a moment of complete and absolute bliss. Certain I had gone to Heaven, my entire body and senses were swept into the beach environment. Feeling I was "home," I fell under the spell of the seagull activity, the sounds and smell of the saltwater, the surfers preparing on the shore, and the surfers in the water testing their skills. My thoughts were going 1,000 directions as the words echoed in my head, *I don't believe I'm in Iowa anymore.*

The saying, "You can never cross the ocean unless you have the courage to lose sight of the shore," was never truer than at the start of this great adventure.

FROM THAT FIRST MOMENT in the surf, the next two years were spent working and playing, totally immersed in the surf, sun, and beach environment of 1969 unspoiled Hawaii.

Weekends were spent with Pat or with my new friends as we explored the sights around the island, from the Pearl Harbor Memorial to all the popular beaches, and at that time, the more secluded beaches to camp—luaus, local food joints, local parties, and 1969 rock concerts.

The Honolulu International Center, known as the HIC, hosted the hottest groups of that era. Being at the right place at the right time was never better for 1969 rock music. My first ever live concert was Sergio Mendes and Brasil 66. Entering the HIC's large venue, it was unbelievable to me that we were in the same building as the musicians, watching them perform live.

Never tiring of all the new experiences, new friends, and the live concert experience of late '60's performances, we grooved to the tunes of Creedence Clearwater Revival, The Doors, and more. As an example, ticket prices at that time for Jimi Hendrix were three dollars and twenty-five cents, and that was top dollar. However, when George Harrison was in town, he was charging nine dollars. No way was I paying that ridiculous amount to see one guy.

I saw Janis Joplin perform at the HIC on July 6, 1970. She died a few months later, on October 4. Her Honolulu concert was considered one of her best live performances, and wow, she did not disappoint.

In the late 1960s, most concerts were sit-down; however, she had the fans on their feet the minute she walked across the stage with her flowing boas, swigging from a bottle of Southern Comfort that she slammed down onto the piano as she passed by on her way to the center stage microphone. At one point, she shouted at the arena security to stand down because if any of the standing fans damaged seats, she would personally pay for them. "Hell," she said as she turned back to the crowd, "I'm even inviting you all to my hotel after the concert for a party!" The crowd went wild as she went on to her next song.

It was tempting to accept the open invite and show up at her hotel for the after-party, but my rural roots rationalized that would cost me two more bus rides. Plus, I had to be at work the next morning. Convincing myself in my typical naiveté—no worries, I would simply catch her party the next time she was in town. I often wonder what might have changed for me had I attended the post-concert party hosted by Janis Joplin.

NEEDING TO IMMEDIATELY generate an income, I accepted an entry-level file clerk position at a large accounting firm in downtown Honolulu. This position paid me three hundred dollars a month, and it was astounding to consider the possibilities of what I could do with all that extra money!

Remember, this was before credit cards were the

norm, so at that point, the majority of society operated cash only. Cash only is a good deterrent to spending unwisely or spending outside the budget. Not that we ever did have that problem, but if the cash ran out, we would simply put off the purchase until the next payday.

Our expenses were uncomplicated—we split the $150 a month rent, which included utilities. TV was free, and we each contributed seven dollars and fifty cents a week for groceries. That fifteen dollars a week fed two people for three meals a day. We were Iowa farm girls, so we knew how to stretch a grocery dollar, plus we had a standard grocery list so we would not exceed our budgeted amount.

We grocery shopped at the local Holiday Mart, which was maybe eight or nine blocks away, a nice Saturday morning walk. After making our purchases, there were always taxis in front of the store, so we would easily catch a cab home. The cab ride home, including tip, was one dollar total.

With no car of my own, I was about to learn how easy it would be for me to commute in this city.

The local bus service for my daily ride to work cost twenty-five cents each way. Having never used public transportation, I learned that commuting every day on a bus filled with strangers was a unique experience. My route was popular with the local working people, and the casual conversations held or overheard while I rode offered another slice of never-ending education into Hawaii local life.

The first time catching the bus from downtown back

to the apartment, I watched as the bus slowed to a stop in front of me at my bus stop and smiled at the large "Waikiki" bus destination indicator on the front of the bus that told me this was "my" bus.

Boarding and dropping my quarter into the fare box, sliding into an empty seat, I quietly giggled and shook my head in giddy disbelief. When, in my wildest dreams, did I ever envision myself working downtown in a city at an accounting firm in an adult job, then riding a public transportation bus emblazoned with "Waikiki" that would take me home after work? Who gets to do that!

Simply amazed at my good fortune, I silently promised myself to never take one single second of this Hawaii experience for granted.

BECAUSE PAT HAD LIVED in Hawaii for a couple of years, she was well established in her work and social life. My past consisted of friends I had known since grade school, so meeting people and making new friends was another fun-added experience. Most of my new friends were met at work, some were met at the beach, and others were introductions or friends of friends.

One new friend was a fellow I dated for a short bit. He was a laundry delivery driver, and the laundry room in the hotel where I worked was on his delivery route. We chatted as he went about his business, and I learned Rich had recently relocated from California to Hawaii.

In no time, he'd asked me out. I had grown up with the boys I had dated in Iowa, so going out with a "complete stranger" was neither comfortable or normal for me, and I declined every day that he asked. He never gave up and was so sweet and sincere, I finally accepted a movie date.

Hanging out after work at his apartment while he changed out of uniform to his everyday clothes, his roommate mentioned Rich's past as a Hell's Angel—I was shocked at that news and his roommate was shocked since he thought I knew that.

Nope, that was a news flash. Sitting on the sofa while he was changing clothes, it suddenly made sense why he was so happy that I accepted his invitation because *Easy Rider* was released that day, and we were going to see it.

I couldn't help but chuckle to myself because here was this rural Iowa gal about to go on a date with a full-on Los Angeles-based Hell's Angel. Nothing like that had ever happened to me before!

In his own home environment, Rich was very relaxed, and I saw a good-looking, fit, heavily tattooed, smart young man. He was very unhappy his roommate shared that information and later explained he didn't talk about that because he was desperate to turn his life around and wanted that to remain in his past.

He eventually admitted he was forced to leave Southern California due to his doing some "business" in the wrong gang's territory, got his ass beaten, nearly died, and was told to leave the state. He shared that meeting me on the first day of his new job, in a new city, bolstered his hopes for a new start.

From that first day we met, he pursued me daily with gentle attention at work. Eventually, I gave him my number, and he called me at home after work. He'd surprise me with small, thoughtful gifts, and we eventually spent time together just sitting by the sea. His mind would drift away on the beach, and he would write poems and musings about love, life, and the ocean. He was definitely getting my attention.

We dated for about a month, and he wrote beautiful thoughts about finally getting into the groove of Hawaii and what it meant to him. He wrote how he had never met anybody like me, and he wrote about spending our lives together and that he planned to marry me. Whoa—that one was totally unexpected.

Then, suddenly, he was gone. I heard nothing from him for several days, and there was a new delivery driver who didn't know Rich; he only knew he had a new route. I felt such a void as I realized how much I missed him.

Calling his apartment, I was finally able to reach his roommate and discovered Rich had abruptly left Hawaii. Apparently Rich's cover had been blown, and he was given "until the next flight" to get off the island by an island gang faction.

His roommate told me Rich was told to not contact anybody and just "go" or face consequences. My heart was broken, but more so for him and his attempt at a new life. His previous life choices had come back to haunt him. I never forgot that as I faced and made certain choices in my young life.

THAT BRIEF TIME WITH RICH opened doors to many other new acquaintances, and I seemed to be meeting many young people from California. The 1960's were a time of great social change and experimentation. Hanging out at the beach with another fellow from Los Angeles, he handed me a funny cigarette. I asked, "What's this?" wondering who buys a crappy looking cigarette like that?

"Here, just take a puff. Not like a cigarette, but inhale and hold it. Haven't you ever smoked pot before?"

Um, no. He explained it would relax me and it would be fun. "Fun." That's all I needed to hear. I inhaled and about choked to death. No, that was *not* fun.

"Here, watch me. Then try it again." Oh, I get it, and he was right. It was relaxing, and it was fun. I also learned it was illegal. And me, do something illegal? Oh, hell no. But, but, but, I looked around and realized that this was the funny smell at concerts. I wondered why people would stealthily pass cigarettes back and forth during the performances. If it was so illegal, why was using it so obvious in Hawaii?

Didn't matter, when I'd hang out with this group, somebody always had some local weed. It wasn't addictive or a "must-have." It was just there and not a big deal.

We made plans to see Led Zeppelin, and I met my friend outside the HIC before the concert. He casually mentioned he didn't score any weed but leaned over, and I saw a small dot of paper about the size of your small fingernail on his pinky finger. He was laughing and said, "But I did find this. Here, take it," as he lightly tapped his pinky finger onto the tip of my tongue.

In all the excitement of going to this concert, I thought that was weird, but oh well. My focus was watching the cast of 1969 hippie characters entering the concert and finding our seats. Finally seated and happily watching the scene around me, I instantly felt what seemed like a bolt of lightning that began in my tailbone, crashed up my spine like a freight train, and exploded in my head.

I turned to him, "Hey, what was that?"

"Oh, that? LSD 25."

WHAT?

I freaked out. I had heard about that stuff, and I had made a pact with myself that there was *no way* was that ever going to enter my body. Not only was I furious at his sneaky and dumb move, but the stuff had just started to kick in.

Seeing and feeling things I'd never seen or felt before, I angrily snapped my head around to look at him. His eyes were "different," and he smiled. "Hey. There's nothing you can do; so you might as well enjoy it."

And just like that, it all made sense.

Realizing he was right, I also started to realize I was not only watching the concert, I was one with it. Yup, he was right, and I knew I would enjoy it.

Boy, did I. Led Zeppelin on acid.

BUT IT GETS BETTER. Since I rode the bus to the HIC, I still had to get myself home. I don't remember how or why or what we did after the concert, but I must have taken the bus down to Waikiki sometime early the next morning because I remember sitting solo on the sands of Waikiki Beach, just before sunrise, amazed at what I had just experienced.

Watching the sun come up over the ocean, I had tears of gratitude, as well as all the emotions tied to the enhanced smells, sounds, and sights of the ocean and that Hawaiian sunrise. Watching, rather being one with that sunrise, I knew my life and view of things was forever changed. And it was good.

Yes, this LSD experience was something I found most entertaining and, over the next twenty years, was able to experience again and again. One thing I learned about psychedelics was that I needed to control the setting in which I started, but then I was good to simply allow the trip to unfold around me.

While in Hawaii, one of my favorite experiences was to head to the beach and day trip by myself, enjoying wonderful adventures, meeting some completely zany 1960's characters, spending hours in Waikiki just people watching, seeing, and partaking of things "dimensionally."

"Dimensionally" to me meant hours of not only listening to music, but it meant I could not only hear, but also see, the music floating on the ocean breezes.

Eating food, like a cookie, I could taste flour, then salt, then nuts—every individual ingredient. Then all those sensations would morph into the incredible experience, or crescendo, of tasting the entire cookie. Experiences like that often just made me giggle.

I tasted the "sunshine" in a slice of pineapple. Who gets to taste sunshine? The first time that happened, I thought I was in Heaven because nothing could ever taste as good as sunshine. I loved sitting in the soft afternoon rain while the sun was shining, which is very common in Hawaii—watching the drops glisten and fall like jewels dripping from the sky. I discovered that everything we normally see is flat, but knowing there are many layers and complexities to the world forced me to think differently because what I normally see is often not the entire picture. Applying that to experiences, conversations, and people helped me better understand why people often say one thing and do another. For some wild reason, it suddenly all made sense. And for fun, I spent hours people watching, or my focus would turn to the swaying palms, or maybe I studied the ocean, often experiencing time at a level that had no words. And it was magical.

By the way, the week after I returned from United 811 was the last time I tripped. I simply had to find a way to "see" what happened to me and better understand it in my head. Rising early one morning, I took a hit of acid, then set about organizing my "nest" in our secluded, tree-filled backyard. Setting up my space included a big, comfy lawn chair lined with a large, warm, fluffy, soft beach towel. I knew I would also need loose, comfy clothing, a hat, and sunglasses.

Settled in, I became transfixed as the sun rose in the cloudless eastern Colorado sky. The breaking dawn took my breath away—my heart filled with gratitude to see the light of this new day.

I observed the sun rise, then it moved from my right, passing over me. I watched the birds in flight, the gentle breezes, the trees moving, and life all around me. As the day began cooling, the sun was on my left side, then dipped into another color-filled Rocky Mountain sunset.

In that moment at the closure of the day, I think I finally took a breath—chuckling quietly to myself, certain I had been holding my breath the entire time. It was all so beautiful—to simply allow the peace-filled day and experience all that life occurring around me was one of the first times I felt safe in many days.

During those twelve, fourteen, sixteen, or whatever number of hours, I never moved from that chair—I did not eat, get anything to drink, go to the bathroom. Nothing in my body moved—only the scattered thoughts banging around in my head. To me, it felt like I had been out there maybe fifteen minutes. Yet, the entire day passed over me while I explored my thoughts and feelings about the incident, and then my life.

As the day turned to dusk, it felt to me that this trip was over. Standing, I stretched, getting my focus while I gathered my things and then moseyed into the house, finally more relaxed and far clearer about "things" than at any time since the incident had happened.

Running a hot bath, scented candles placed around the tub and the bathroom, I lowered my still battered and aching body into the warm water and deeply inhaled the scented air—suddenly smiling as I realized, *Oh, hell no. We're not done here yet with this adventure,* and welcomed the new sensations and revelations that were once again washing over me.

Why do I no longer expose myself to psychedelics? I don't trust that I will find and ingest something pure because today's culture is not about "grooving." It is a harsher drug culture. I came from a time of freeing and chilling out, not "I gotta do this." That was not me; I was not a "druggie." I simply enjoyed enhancing experiences whereas today's drug culture is intent on escaping experiences.

Swiss scientist Dr. Albert Hofmann described it this way when he accidently discovered LSD, "I suddenly became strangely inebriated. The external world became changed, as in a dream. Objects appeared to gain in relief; they assumed unusual dimensions; and colors became more glowing. Even self-perception and the sense of time were changed. When the eyes were closed, colored pictures flashed past in a quickly changing kaleidoscope. After a few hours, the not unpleasant inebriation, which had been experienced while I was fully conscious, disappeared. What had caused this condition?"

However, self-medicating in other ways became an integral part of my life and coping mechanisms during the rapidly approaching bumpy times.

June, 1969. Shari's introduction to the Pacific Ocean and Hawaiian beach life.

Christmas, 1970. Shari and Pat in front of our Christmas tree and big jalousie window wall of our small Honolulu apartment.

Chapter Six

ARRIVING IN HAWAII IN JUNE 1969 placed me in a perfect position to witness the history making July 16, 1969, Apollo 11 moon mission. This momentous NASA space flight was under the command of Commander Neil Armstrong and crewed by Edwin "Buzz" Aldrin and Michael Collins. After the historic launch, I spent many hours sitting on the stairs outside our apartment front door simply gazing at the moon, contemplating the extraordinary event the world was witnessing.

The astronauts launched on July 16, landing four days later on the moon's surface. Commander Neil Armstrong and Buzz Aldrin were the first humans on the moon.

The flight successfully returned on July 24 splashing down 920 miles southwest of Hawaii and thirteen miles from the recovery ship, the USS *Hornet*. For health reasons, once on board the recovery ship, the astronauts were secured in a mobile quarantine station.

Two days later, July 26, the astronauts arrived in Hawaii to be transported and were then quarantined in a NASA trailer as a precaution against any possible germs or disease they may have brought with them from the moon.

On July 27, a welcome home ceremony was planned at Pearl Harbor. Pat's friend Lee, a US Navy sailor stationed there, invited me to attend the parade and celebration with him. Knowing Pearl Harbor well, Lee and I arrived early, parked, and walked the short distance from the car to the parade route.

Once again, the timing was flawless.

Before crossing the street to continue our shortcut to the parade route, we paused on a vacant backstreet corner to get our bearings. We knew the streets were blocked off for the parade, so we were surprised to hear nearby traffic. Puzzled, we looked to our right as a large vehicle pulling a flatbed rounded the corner, turning directly toward us.

As it passed in front of us, we saw a large silver trailer firmly anchored on the flatbed. Stunned at the unusual sight, we watched, astonished to notice three smiling faces pressed to the small trailer windows. Lee and I gasped, grabbed each other's arm, and at the same time, cried out, "OMG, that's the astronauts!"

We quickly realized we had stumbled into the staging area (likely a high security sector, but there we were), and their rig was being positioned here behind the scenes, prior to the parade.

With maybe a dozen other people in the area, it was clear the astronauts were looking directly at us. Absolutely thrilled, Lee and I began excitedly waving with both hands, and they waved back. Hastily removing my small Brownie camera from my bag, I began taking photos as fast as I could as they slowly passed. The astronauts rolled out of sight, and we were speechless, humbled, and absolutely giddy to have enjoyed a private wave and moment with our newest American space heroes.

NOTES/APOLLO 11:

From Pearl Harbor, NASA transported the trailer housing the quarantined astronauts to Houston where they finally emerged after three weeks in isolation.

Two little known facts—The Apollo 11 crew recognized the possibility they might not return safely, leaving their families with little financial support. Because of the extreme danger of this assignment, they didn't qualify or take out life insurance. Rather, they signed hundreds of autographs in the chance they didn't return home, their families would have been able to sell them. Fortunately, the autographs weren't needed for financial support;

however, they often turn up at auctions sometimes selling for as much as $30,000.

Even the Apollo 11 astronauts are required go through customs to reenter the United States. According to the customs form filed at the Honolulu Airport on July 24, 1969, the astronauts declared moon rocks, moon dust, and various lunar samples. The form, signed by all three astronauts, showed they declared their cargo and listed their flight route as beginning at Cape Kennedy (now Cape Canaveral) with a stopover on the moon.

WORKING FULL-TIME at the accounting firm through the rest of the summer, filing documents and running errands around downtown, I was often found wandering in the cement jungle of downtown Honolulu as I worked to get my bearings. Even though this was all so new to me, I felt I was finally finding my groove. On the Friday of the week of my three-month work anniversary, my boss called me to his office, where he terminated my employment, effective that day.

He explained management decided to let two of the file clerks go and fill the positions with one recent college graduate holding an accounting degree. Devastated to receive a pink slip and final check on a Friday afternoon, it felt like I had been hit by a truck.

Taking my final check and thanking him for the opportunity, I headed to my bus stop. Boarding the bus, stunned and numb, riding home, I could barely drag myself up the three flights of stairs. Slowly entering our apartment, I sat quietly, contemplating my options until Pat came home from her work.

By this time, I was convinced nobody would ever hire someone who had been fired. After all, my small-town, work-hard, figure-it-out, do-your-best nature could not grasp why a business would ever fire a good employee. So, guess what that made me?

Concluding all that, my stubborn side determined it might just be time for me to return to Iowa. I dreaded telling my family the horror of losing my job, I was as low as I'd ever been, and all the wind was blown out of my sails for sure.

Pat quietly and patiently listened to my self-imposed butt-kicking, then talked me off the ledge, convincing me the termination was not a direct reflection on me or made me a bad employee; it was rather a management decision to combine two entry-level positions into one position.

Her suggestion was to think Hawaiian-style. First, no sad face, enjoy the weekend! On Monday, find a new, fun, local job. Enough with the serious; have some fun here!

Pat's view of the situation certainly cheered me up. Her suggestion became my new Plan B. Following a fun weekend at the beach, first thing Monday morning, I went out for a newspaper, and right in front of me in the help wanted ads was the answer—an ad seeking employees for the newly formed housekeeping department of a recently constructed Waikiki hotel.

The property was the Queen Kapiolani Hotel, located on Kapahulu Avenue across from Waikiki Beach. They were in the process of new construction cleanup, which would be followed by room set up, and then the grand opening. As it was nearing opening day, they were hiring many people.

My first day on the job was spent training on room cleaning procedures, with the expectation of cleaning up to fifteen rooms per day.

At the conclusion of the one-day training, there was no question I would search out the boss to discuss what other positions were available. Luckily, an option was an easy transfer to help staff the hotel laundry room, and I jumped on it. Once again, someone was watching over me.

The next day, entering the hotel's lower level parking lot location to get to the laundry room, I was greeted by my new work partner, Kealoha. This grace-filled, happy, hula-dancing, local gal was twenty-five years my senior and became a remarkable mentor to me.

Our "job" was laundry. We were responsible for laundering and stocking each floor's linen closets for this new 312-room property. Here I learned another something new about myself. I discovered this laundry room work was my dream job. I love, love, love to do laundry!

The hotel provided hideous mustard colored button front dresses as our staff uniforms. A typical day was a bus ride from the apartment through the Waikiki scene, and then to be dropped off at the end of Waikiki Beach near the hotel.

It was a short half block walk to hotel, then down to the garage level to enter the laundry area. A quick change into the uniform and off I'd go to help stock the maids' carts with fresh linens, bathroom soaps, and shampoos, plus cleaning supplies. When the guests went about their business or checked out, the rooms were cleaned. As the day went on, the sheets and towels would start pouring in from the laundry chutes above. The remainder of the day, we laundered, dried, and folded load after load of white linens and towels.

At days' end, we would change back into civilian clothes and I would walk the half block from the hotel back to the Waikiki Beach front bus stop. Standing at the edge of the beach, taking in the scene of people enjoying the late afternoon sun, I might wander down to the water's edge to dip my toes into the water or go on in and swim. Later, refreshed and relaxed, I'd catch the bus for the short ride home.

The locals on this route were typically hospitality employees and younger local kids who spent the day on the beach and were either going home, or to their night shift in a restaurant, or to their entertainment jobs in Waikiki.

Kealoha and I spent all day talking and laughing while we were "working." She loved sharing Hawaii stories and would often demonstrate hula moves, explaining the song and the hand motions' mystical meanings.

She loved showing and teaching me ancient Hawaiian culture and shared her Hawaiian-style humor.

When she was sharing Hawaiian stories, Kealoha simply glowed as she transformed from a laundry room employee to an ancient Hawaiian Elder. Her face softened, and her eyes assumed a dreamy, faraway look as her voice slipped into the melodic sing song cadence of an ancient, revered and mystical Elder. She often lost herself in the stories, speaking beautifully and eloquently about Hawaiian history—how, as a child, she walked the relatively empty Waikiki beaches after school. She could describe the beautiful foliage and open spaces I had imagined I would see from my airplane arrival to Hawaii—instead those open areas were filled with high-rises and commerce.

She shared her experiences when Pearl Harbor was bombed on December 7, 1941, and all through WWII, and about the work of Hawaiian Elders, who were doing their utmost to maintain Hawaiian values in the children, even though they were being influenced by the West and Hawaii's booming tourist trade. She talked of the sacred spaces on the different islands and the ancient stories about Menehunes, the little people of Hawaiian mythology. She spoke reverently of the Hawaiians' respect for Pele, the goddess of fire, lightening, wind, and volcanoes, and the creator of the Hawaiian Islands. She shared tales of many other Hawaiian deities and renowned Kahunas, ancient Hawaiian wise men and women, or shamans.

Listening to her melodic voice as we worked made the time fly. She would often gently sway as she folded and stacked a table full of fluffy towels, softly singing Hawaiian songs, then translating them for me. She was unable to stop herself from including the hula hand gestures as she fell under the spell, reminiscing about ancient Hawaiian gods, goddesses, and myths, retelling the old stories she had been taught by her wise Hawaiian healers and Elders.

As the only *haole* (a person who is not a native Hawaiian, especially a Caucasian) who worked in housekeeping and one of the few haoles on the entire property staff, Kealoha watched out for me. She helped my integration with the locals working there by introducing me to everyone as her friend. Highly respected among the staff, her recognizing me with such an honor carried great weight with those working there. My respect and admiration for her knew no bounds.

Two years later, when I was leaving Hawaii to return to the mainland, Pat invited Kealoha and Malama, another Hawaiian friend, to join us for my goodbye dinner at a local landmark revolving restaurant in Waikiki called The Top of Waikiki. After dinner, Kealoha invited me to join her for a last, private moment. Kealoha paid me one of the highest compliments when she took my hands in hers, looked me square in the eyes, and softly shared, "You have Hawaiian heart. You will return some day."

Kealoha was a hard worker, an amazing Hawaiian historian, and ornery as heck! Those Hawaiians have a bawdy sense of humor and love a party. She shared that the ancient Kahunas often drank for two days, recovered for one more, THEN would work on the issue the villagers summoned them to address!

So yes, we enjoyed the crazy stuff too. And believe me, there were some characters in the house. She knew them well, their families and their history. Oh, the times I'd laugh until I cried at her stories.

Our group rounded out when four young local guys joined us in our work responsibilities. Those fellows were charged with handling the heavy lifting around the housekeeping department. Because of our vast range of duties, we all carried master room keys. When we became bored or needed a break, the boys and I would search the daily hotel room roster for vacant rooms. Finding one facing Waikiki Beach, we would wander off to meet up in the room. We would move directly to the ocean view balcony to enjoy the scenery and just let time pass by. The sun would be shining while we relaxed in the patio chairs, discussing whatever with our bare feet up on the balcony railing. Discussions usually ended with me typically the recipient of another version of Hawaii education from another generation, this time on surfing or where to find the best local, Hawaiian food. For eighteen months, we fully enjoyed this fun group who worked hard and looked out for each other. It was the dream job that perfectly fit my plan to change it up and work a fun, local job.

RESORT HOTEL WORK often created some strange situations and certainly instances that would likely never occur in or around Alburnett, Iowa. One day, police descended on the hotel with full lights and blaring sirens in response to the report of a young woman being badly beaten in her hotel room.

Longer term guests often became fixtures and were people we would get to know. In this case, we were uncertain of this woman's story, as this *haole* guest was very private. She was often alone, although occasionally with a man. She was very young, maybe late teens or early twenties, with long brown hair usually up in a ponytail. She dressed Hawaiian casual, often projecting a sad, please-don't-bother-me air about her.

Of course, we respected that, and when I saw her on property, I would greet her with a smile. With a tilt of her head, she often offered back a shy, sideways half-smile— her eyes telling me she would like, even need, a friend. Yet, she deliberately kept us all at a distance.

On this day, we watched as the first responders removed her from the hotel to an ambulance. As they brought her through the lobby, it was clear she took the worst of a horrible fight.

Of course, at this point, housekeeping stepped in to methodically deep clean the room. When the boys flipped the mattress, we discovered a worn and tear-stained spiral notebook journal stuffed between the mattress and box spring.

I gently opened it, searching for a name or contact info. However, what I stumbled across was page after page of handwritten musings that exposed this young lady's story.

By the looks of it, she spent hours writing about her life. She wrote she was the new wife of her hometown sweetheart. She wrote about falling in love with this boy who had evolved into the brave and honor-filled soldier she loved deeply.

Her soldier served in Viet Nam and returned to her badly injured, paralyzed, and unable to walk. In their dark hour, she wrote of their hopes for the future and for starting a family. The writing turned to a sudden, unexpected, life-changing day, and then she wrote of his return and their fears surrounding their new life.

In her anguish, she wrote of their financial worries, how they needed money to get home and start over, how they addressed the issue of her being their sole support, his torment at her suggesting and him agreeing that prostitution was the only way she could make a lot of money fast and get them set up back at home.

Unsure what to do with my emotions, I stopped reading. I took deep breaths to steady myself because, at that point, I was becoming unable to continue reading through my tears.

After a few minutes, I went on reading her words.

She described her attempts to comprehend the incredible pain of this, their new life. She wrote how with every trick she turned, her focus must remain on the fact she loved her soldier more than she hated what she was doing.

She wrote how she would return from this hotel room to the safety of her soldier after "work." She wrote of his love and concern for her *knowing* what she had just done for them. He would simply hold her. Sometimes she remained quiet, seldom sharing her day's experiences; mostly, she cried. As strong and brave as she described him, she also described how he often fought it, yet his emotions would overflow, and he would hold and cry with her.

Only once did he cry out and angrily shout through his tears. He let out his anguish that he loved her so much and he couldn't give her what she got by selling herself. He never spoke of it again.

Every day, as she left her soldier, she placed a lingering kiss in the middle of his forehead. They agreed to offer no parting words, as they both knew how she spent her days in this hotel room.

I felt raw, not believing what I had just read. Gathering myself and my thoughts, I located the authorities investigating the matter and handed them the notebook. Walking away, my head was spinning; this girl looked and sounded about my age. With my "Mayberry" upbringing, a situation such as this wasn't anywhere on my radar, and my heart ached for them.

This also explained seeing her either alone or with a man. We never saw her or heard anything more. After the severe beating by one of her clients, she either didn't survive, or they simply left Hawaii. Still today, she often crosses my mind.

ANOTHER INCIDENT INVOLVED one of the house-keepers, Yoshiko, the mother of two adult children. Yoshiko spoke only Japanese and endured an arranged marriage with a brutish Norwegian Merchant Marine. Yoshiko kept to herself—until the day she shared a portion of her story with another housekeeper.

She spilled her story of a dangerous marriage where she was badly abused. Her injuries were never exposed because he was good at beating her where it would not show. Her children witnessed this for years and begged her to leave him. She could not, as he warned her that if she left, he would find her and kill her. He had her fully convinced that she could not leave him or she would die. This day, she was troubled, as she shared that she had lost the respect of her children.

Western culture often does not realize the serious-ness of this loss of respect. In her culture, losing re-spect was far more intense than suffering shame. It can be like losing one's place in life. Complete loss of respect is equivalent to full exile—you become a non-person, even to family or close friends. You often can't speak or be spoken to, be heard or seen. You are just not present.

This personal information was unknown to any of the rest of us that day.

While working my usual laundry shift, there was a faint sound heard over the hum of the washers and dryers. Unsure what it was or if I even really heard anything, I dismissed it. Then there was another, slightly louder and longer noise. It sounded like a moan and was only slightly more audible over the background noise.

Stepping out into the attached open-air, underground parking lot, I wondered if that sound was from a nearby injured animal. Walking around the corner, following the moaning sounds, I saw Yoshiko lying on the ground, crumpled and badly contorted.

Seeing her like that stopped me in my tracks. I was baffled as it appeared her back, legs, and arms were all misshapen. A sick feeling descended as it dawned on me -- she was misshapen because her bones were broken! How did that happen—was she pushed off her floor, or had she jumped?

Running over to her, it was clear this was not good. Screaming for help from anybody in the work area, I raced into the hotel to get authorities, while everybody at reception sprang into action.

We were unsure what to do while waiting for the first responders because moving her was not an option. She was very badly injured and struggling to breath. The Japanese-speaking employees were leaning over and stroking her face, softly talking to her as she was immediately bundled into the ambulance.

We later learned she did not survive the severe internal, head, and bodily injuries. Well-liked, humble, kind, hardworking, dependable Yoshiko was dead, and everyone was shaken to their core.

MY SHIFT THAT DAY was scheduled to end at nine p.m., however, all the other housekeepers on duty simply gathered their belongings and silently walked off the job that afternoon. Kealoha had checked out earlier in the day, but she came back to the property when she heard the news.

She and I spoke quietly as she explained the housekeepers would not return until the property was blessed and cleansed by Reverend Akaka, a well-known and beloved local Hawaiian spiritual advisor.

My next words I share are meant with no disrespect to Yoshiko or my Hawaiian friends. These words come from a place of how I was raised and experienced life and death. What Kealoha shared with me regarding Hawaiian traditions, I did not know.

I thought she was kidding.

I could not get my head around the fact the staff just walked off the job and everybody was OK with that? They can stay away until some local tribal shaman comes back to bless the land?

My puzzled look and silence encouraged Kealoha to

continue with this new information and the Hawaiian view of passing. Now that nearly every local had left the building, she, too, returned home.

Alone in the lower level of the hotel, I struggled to adjust to not only the events of the day and this strange new information but then the eerie quiet with most of the staff gone. Moving to sit by the open laundry room doorway to capture a slight breeze, something compelled me to get up, board the service elevator, and push "7"—the floor Yoshiko had worked.

The doors of the elevator opened on the seventh floor. That sixth sense continued drawing me into the open-air hallway to the area where she likely jumped. Turning the corner, I stopped in my tracks at the sight of a single armless chair, the metal back pushed up against the railing.

Gasping, I realized this was clearly the ledge and location she chose to plunge to her death.

Abruptly, the air around me shifted, creating the perception I was no longer alone in the hallway. Cautiously stepping slowly and deliberately toward that lone chair, my feelings were simply overwhelmed. Feeling bewildered and perplexed, I was caught up in my thoughts, contemplating her most likely final moments.

Clearly from the heartbreaking drama laid out before me, this was no accident. She deliberately searched out a chair, carried it to this spot, and pushed it up against the railing as she made her final decision to step up and launch herself over the seven-story-high railing.

The crushing sensation of despair, loss, loneliness, a sense of worthlessness, sadness, anger, and tears welled up in me as I was slowly drawn toward the solitary chair.

I stopped, staring, barely breathing, fixated at the entire scene, my senses, again, completely overwhelmed as I wondered how dreadful life's circumstances would be that a person could plan and execute something as absolute as she had.

A small, internal voice began to nudge me, telling me it was OK to go ahead and check out this area. Gently and convincingly the mantra in my head repeatedly told me it was OK to come forward into the space. It was OK for me to step up on the chair, to see what it looked like below, to peer over the ledge, it was not that far down.

Totally drawn in, hearing this and entranced with it all, I suddenly stepped back. My heart pounded as I realized these were not my thoughts. I had no death wish—what was this all about?

Turning quickly, I willed myself to get out of there. Racing straight to the service elevator, repeatedly jabbing the basement floor button, I finally let out a huge sigh of relief as the door on the seventh floor closed. Standing alone, I stared as that creaking elevator moved downward until it opened to deposit me back into the quiet sanctuary of the laundry room.

Bolting from the elevator in one swift motion, I grabbed my stuff and left. Those past few minutes had been beyond creepy and felt very wrong.

Boarding the bus for my ride home, I was lost in my thoughts. I was bewildered about this sudden bizarre and otherworldly experience, which propelled me to escape from the hotel as fast as I could.

Prior to going in at noon for my next day's shift, I called the hotel receptionist to ask if Reverend Akaka had arrived. The relieved receptionist told me yes, he arrived early, blessed the entire property, and offered an extended blessing for all who entered there. Reassured, I asked her if the staff had returned and was told yes, the people had returned to work. Hanging up, satisfied that since the locals were back on board to enter the recently cleansed property, I, too, was all in.

My shift began uneventfully. However, for several days following this episode, when I utilized the service elevator, after I pressed any floor button to the upper floors, the elevator *always* stopped on "7."

The elevator doors would slowly creak open to an empty hallway where I could see nobody was standing there, and then the doors slowly closed. Asking around, I determined none of the other staff experienced this or any other phantom-like encounters.

The first day the elevator stopped at "7" on its own, as the door fully opened, I felt an unnatural, ghostly, and otherworldly coolness enter the space and surround me. Each time after that, when the elevator stopped at "7" and I felt the air moving around me, even as creepy as it was, I wondered with a slight chuckle, *Hmmm, did someone or something just get on the elevator—or just get off?*

For days after this event, while riding the bus to and from work, I would reflect on the local Hawaiians' strong belief system in spiritual cleansing of the property versus my hesitancy to embrace such a concept. Perhaps my lack of knowledge on this and my uncertainty caused me to feel the unnatural and uncomfortable stirrings around me. Perhaps those with their strong Hawaiian faith moved on relatively unaffected and maybe even protected. This was another hey-wait-justa-minute-here experience that prodded me to ponder other life and afterlife possibilities I had not previously considered during my basic Methodist upbringing.

AFTER MORE THAN A YEAR working at the Queen Kapiolani Hotel, a department management shakeup created significant issues, causing many to leave for other jobs.

Checking my options, I determined "fun jobs" don't always completely pay the bills, and I turned my focus to my next position, in the office of a local trust company in downtown Honolulu. Kealoha and I remained good friends, and I made it a point to spend time with her whenever I returned to visit Hawaii.

July, 1969. Pearl Harbor parade honoring the Apollo Astronauts. Notice the deserted streets in this staging area. In the far right window of the silver trailer, you can see the face and waving hand of one of the astronauts. He's looking right at us and waving. We were so excited, I can't believe I had the presence of mind to find my camera and shoot this quick photo!

Chapter Seven

FROM HAWAII BACK TO THE MAINLAND
1971

LOOKING BACK ON THE approximately 100 week-ends I spent living in and fully enjoying the land of Aloha's surf, sun and seafood vibes, plus live '60s music, I was beginning to feel the draw to return to the mainland and, specifically, Iowa.

Early one morning, I received a long-distance call from Mother-Vic. My railroad engineer dad was involved in a major head-on train accident, and she had her hands full. That easily finalized my decision to leave Hawaii and head home to help during his recovery.

My prime focus was to help around the house as his broken bones mended. As he fully recovered from significant, albeit nonlife-threatening injuries, my thoughts turned to, *Where do I go from here?*

I had left a small Iowa farm community three weeks out of high school and immersed myself in the late 1960s Hawaii, and then I returned home two years later. To say things changed for me is a complete understatement.

While helping at home, I also took a job at a local area bank. After my unexpected job dismissal in Hawaii, I was determined to seek work outside of my comfort level, and in whatever industry I chose, I would apply to work at only the "best" in that industry.

In my self-education, I wanted to learn from the best, be inspired, and be exposed to new things. It made sense, and that way, I would never get in a job rut. Working in this large Cedar Rapids bank was my first step in that direction.

Content to spend time with old friends, I also made many new friends at work. After nearly a year back in Iowa, and after a shocking reminder of how brutal Iowa winters can be, my sense of longing to return to water and a beach lifestyle overtook me.

My restless eagerness to expand and explore my new adult life lead me to reach out to Ted, a Hawaii friend who served in the US Air Force and was stationed at the sleepy (well, it was early 1970's) beach town of Panama City, Florida. Ted often mentioned that when I was ready to return to beach life, I had an open invitation to move in with him and his roommate in Panama City.

Now ready to move, I talked with Scott, an old high school friend who was packing up to return to Florida for college with two of his buddies. They were driving straight through to Miami, if I wanted to ride along and share driving and expenses. Oh, how I love a good road trip!

In less than two weeks, I resigned from my job, packed up my few belongings, said my goodbyes, and joined the guys on the 1,500-plus miles and twenty-four-plus hours, straight through drive from Iowa to Miami, Florida.

Meeting up for the early morning launch to Florida, Scott introduced me to his friends. We worked to secure our few belongings in the trunk or any available nook and cranny of the car, each carving out space for our seats, and off we went. The trip was uneventful as we took turns driving, gassing up, grabbing a snack, and trying to sleep between driving shifts.

Nothing rowdy; this was not a party train. Rather, it was put the pedal to the metal and point it south. Destination: Miami and their college after they stopped long enough to drop me in Tallahassee to catch a Greyhound to my destination—Panama City.

Landing in Tallahassee, I called Ted to make arrangements to meet at the Panama City Greyhound station. Hanging up the phone to board the bus, I was getting a second wind with the excitement of finally returning to the beach.

TED WAS WAITING at the Panama City bus station

and helped load my meager belongings into his car. Leaving the terminal, catching my first glimpse of the Florida Panhandle, all I could do was chuckle to myself as, once again, this part of Florida was not at all what I expected to see.

This was not South Beach; this was the Deep South! Deep South as in this geography was everglades and a mild climate ideal for birds, alligators, turtles, and snakes. *What?* Naively, once again, somehow believing all beach communities were Hawaiian tropical, this swampy subtropical wilderness was not at all what I had envisioned.

Ted lived in a rented bright yellow fifty-five-foot by ten-foot mobile home off base in a piney, wooded mobile home park that he shared with Jim, an Air Force buddy. Yes, you can almost hear the banjos playing in the background.

From bouncing down the interstates in that tightly packed car, then over three hours on a Greyhound bus, having no good sleep, junk food, and little water, when we finally reached their mobile home, my body was nearly delirious with exhaustion.

The mobile home was in fairly good condition in spite of the harsh, humid Florida weather conditions. Parking on the sand next to the only side door, entering the home deposited me directly into the small, carpeted living room. The dark paneled room boasted a shabby, comfortable sofa and one reclining chair. To my right, the living room carpet revealed a well-worn path to the

dated yellowed linoleum floor of the compact kitchen/
dining room. To my left were Ted and Jim's two small
bedrooms and the one tiny bathroom, all of fifty-five
feet, front to back. Privacy was never going to be my
issue here—there was none!

Always the good host and seeing my fatigue, Ted
pulled out the sofa bed in the middle of the living room/
dining room/kitchen and tossed fresh bedding on top of
the pullout. I made the bed in a near catatonic state and
could not wait to crawl under the clean sheets. By then, I
was so tired, I wondered if sleep was even possible. After
seeing my new surroundings for the first time, my body
slowly relaxed and moved toward the much-needed rest.
Meanwhile, my brain would not stop whirling, considering what to do with this, my next adventure.

Once I finally fell into welcome sleep, Ted's roommate,
Jim, came home from work. He entered through the door
that opened right about where my head was on the pullout
sofa. He walked in, nearly on top of me, jarring me out
of a deep sleep. There was no sleeping with all the activity
going on around me. His demeanor quickly proved that
while my friend Ted thought me moving in and helping
with rent and expenses was a good idea, Jim did not.

Jim was clear from the get-go that their place was
not big enough for three. Even though I tried my darned-
est to be helpful and/or just get out of the way, clearly,
me sleeping on the sofa in the tiny living room area, my
stuff in the bathroom, me in the small kitchen, or me

anywhere around the property was one of the many reasons Jim and I often butted heads. Even moving outside to sit on the steps was an issue, as the mobile homes were parked so close together you could hear everything going on with the neighbors. Awkward.

Combined with the huge quantity and variety of Florida's enormous bugs, the heat, and the humidity, just sitting outside in general Florida swamp conditions was not appealing.

One evening, Jim walked in carrying a single steak for his dinner. With little acknowledgment I was even there, he began cooking. I scooted out of his way; I was just not up for any drama.

Repositioning myself as far from the kitchen as possible, Jim reluctantly asked me to help him get the old, temperamental kitchen stove to work. Sighing and thinking, *Oh, here we go,* I pulled up my big girl britches and moseyed over to see what was going on.

We were both surprised to discover that with my willingness to assist and successfully coaxing that old stove to work, any resistance and annoyance Jim had shown me relating to my intrusion into their tiny space was no longer an issue.

I understood this was his home too. Plus, I understood his irritation when his friend dropped this goofy hippie chick he met in Hawaii into their home, plopping her onto the sofa and into their lives. All that change did not sit with this traditional, Midwestern, outdoorsy guy.

This time, because we were working together instead of him being surly and nitpicky, he became helpful, chatty, friendly, and funny. We married six months later.

A FEW MONTHS AFTER the wedding, feeling restless, I became even more focused on returning to the casual, tropical beach life. Sharing stories of endless sun, surf, and sand with Jim gradually helped him warm to the idea of moving our small family, which included two German Shepherds, Sandy and Leon, to California.

As soon as he transitioned out of the Air Force, we packed up our few personal belongings and drove our van from Florida to his hometown, nestled along the woodsy shores of Lake Michigan. We spent four long winter months there with his family, enduring a teeth-chattering, bitterly cold Michigan winter.

During our time in Michigan, I found a job at a local retail outlet. Jim hunted deer for food, in appreciation of his family housing us, did chores around the house, and built out our small van to include a better bed across the back and additional storage areas, including a small pantry and makeshift portable, outdoor kitchen, easily accessed when we opened the van's back cargo doors. It was not an ideal food prep arrangement in bad weather, but it worked well otherwise. To further downsize, we discarded a few more of the obvious, nonessential items. We repacked our things, loaded Sandy and Leon, and began the drive west, which took us through Colorado.

Missing our exit to our original destination, Boulder, we found ourselves in Denver.

After four months in the cold and windy gusts blowing over frozen Lake Michigan, then driving I-80 West across icy and windblown Iowa and Nebraska highways, the suddenly mild high desert of sunny, low humidity Denver weather was a welcome relief.

Humans and canines alike all came alive in the crisp, fresh Denver air. After the cloudy gray days and pitch dark, frosty nights of the Midwest winter, we welcomed the cloudless blue skies and majestic Rocky Mountain snowcapped peaks rising over this beautiful city.

Rather than continue our journey as a road race to California, we agreed to slow down, enjoy and explore this new part of the country. Jim suggested the van undergo minor engine work prior to tackling a high-altitude Rocky Mountain crossing enroute to California.

While out and about, we met people willing to work a trade for the van's repairs. We also followed suggestions of areas to explore, and we became more familiar with the territory.

Exploring and playing during the day, we walked the dogs in parks to watch the sun set, waiting until after dark to pull into secluded church parking lots or remain near many beautiful city parks. It was glorious to be in the middle of winter, yet able to roll out at daybreak to walk the dogs in the mild temperature as the sun came up.

We showered when and where we could at Ys or at

the local rec centers. We spent many days exploring the city parks, mountain trails, and small mountain communities, which were all freeing and great fun after the structured military life and living with the in-laws for four months.

Each day, we woke up to near-perfect weather, and we simply allowed the days to unfold, pulling over to fix a meal, feed, water, and play with the dogs. Late afternoons, we would discover a new place to camp for the evenings. Nearly every day was our personal tailgating party, and then one day, we realized we had spent over three weeks living on the streets of Denver in the van.

Because we had no schedule or destination once we reached California, our idea of staying in Denver before moving further west evolved into: "Maybe we should stay put a while longer." Taking stock of our dwindling finances and seeing we had nothing left to sell or trade, we needed to earn some money for food and gas. With full agreement and a sense of adventure, we decided it was time to rent a place with a real address for at least a year. And just like that, we were Denver residents!

Jim and I were married for just under two years. During our marriage, we faced the usual adjustment from a regulated military atmosphere to a more unfettered civilian situation. The new civilian environment outside the USAF exposed the vastly different views we each held of our future life. This crossroads of me spontaneously suggesting "turn right" and Jim seeking to stay the course by "going left" placed an irreparable strain on the relationship. We divorced.

DIVORCE! Nobody in my family was divorced. I gave my word, and I meant it when I vowed to him standing in church, in front of my family, his family, and our minister, "'til death do us part." Did this make me a liar, which was totally against everything I was taught growing up?

We were both stunned at this turn of events. Jim withdrew from everything relating to our life. Not only was I blindsided by this situation, I was sick to my stomach that our seemingly happy and carefree life plan had turned suddenly into this.

Neither one of us could grasp how to navigate this rocky time, beginning with sorting through all the emotions. My heart was broken and sad that this kind, compassionate, gentle man and I would no longer be sharing our lives.

Day after day of no sleep, I was barely eating and simply making myself go through the motions. We spent endless days in deep, emotional pain while attempting to grasp the enormous sense of loss, disappointment, sadness, confusion, and frustration. Making the decision to end this marriage was emotionally devastating to both of us. Never had I felt so lost or hurt this badly.

Slowly picking up the pieces, I willed myself out of the isolation I created to protect my heart. My self-preservation instincts had kicked in, forcing me to feel "nothing" in this isolated state because when I allowed myself to feel anything, all I could feel was pain.

My new Denver friends gradually convinced me to spend a little bit of time with them. One of the gang was Mark, a fellow Iowan Pat knew and had dated in Hawaii. What was the chance he, too, landed in Colorado? We shared great times in Hawaii, and it was good to see him when we ran into each other back here on the mainland.

Over the following year, we began seeing more and more of each other through mutual friends, and we eventually rented a house with another transplanted Iowa friend. For the next two years, the three of us enjoyed countless fun times entertaining, traveling, or camping nearly every weekend exploring Colorado. Our small family unit slowly evolved as Mark and I became more serious about our relationship, and we eventually purchased our own home and married.

Mark was also a product of a small Iowa community, and we discovered similar backgrounds and interests relating to our families and extended families. Our various family members met when visiting our home, and on each visit, became better acquainted.

Mark was very intelligent, so when he saw an opportunity to start his own business, he took it and grew the business through his imagination, persistence, ingenuity, and working long hours.

We were still living in Denver, and with his new,

rapidly expanding business venture, it became clear that returning to my beach life was no longer on the radar. My Plan B became finding a way to travel to the beach often and inexpensively. Then it hit me, *I'll work for an airline!* A travel industry job would allow us to travel regularly, plus Denver's Stapleton Airport was growing rapidly and evolving into a major airline hub, so the airlines were hiring.

During this period, I worked with several different airline carriers, and their generous travel benefits took us to weekends on the coast and exploring new cities all over the country. Mark was also loving the freedom provided by these travel perks, and this exciting environment perfectly suited his energetic, charming, fun, and adventure-seeking nature.

He arranged a three-day weekend jaunt to New Orleans with a goal of drinking in every bar on Bourbon Street. Mission accomplished, plus we hit a few local hot spots on the side streets.

On this trip, we were about to wrap up one of our fun evenings, and the restaurant staff was setting up an area at the end of the bar with party streamers and balloons. Mark asked for the check to settle up, and the bartender leaned over to ask, "Where are you two going!" followed with an invite to a staffer's birthday party that would start in a few hours at four a.m. Of course, Mark never wanted to miss a party, and what an authentic New Orleans hoedown that turned out to be.

We enjoyed monthly three-day weekend winter jaunts to Puerto Vallarta. Leaving Denver at nine a.m., we were comfortably seated at the pool bar of our favorite hotel by one p.m. We were greeted by our hotel staff friends, who arranged prime seating to enjoy beachside tropical beverages, the freshest seafood, and glorious ocean sunsets.

We often returned to Hawaii to enjoy the hospitality on the less touristy outer islands.

Our days were full of friends, parties, family, travel, and work.

As Mark's manufacturing business grew, the marriage became strained. While Mark remains one of the most intelligent people I have ever met, when he was "on," he was oh-so-charming, generous, funny, a creative chef, and a gracious host, full of great ideas for fun and the life of the party. Other days? He was a perfectionist, controlling, angry, impatient, a bully, and mean.

Most people, myself included, often wondered why a spouse would stay with someone who treated them badly. I guess I needed to experience it myself so I could understand.

When Mark and I met in the late '60s, we were young and active, always seeking the next fun time. While living in the rental with our Iowa friend, our Friday nights after work would start when the three of us pooled our pocket change to buy a $1.83 six pack of Olympia beer. Or we would spontaneously load up whomever else was at the house and head to the local mountain saloon featuring live music and twenty-five-cent shots of Jose Cuervo or Jack Daniels, leaving only when they closed the place. Or we would create fabulous food using whatever we found in the cupboard or from leftovers in the fridge. We'd invite friends over and party until dawn. We had no worries, and we were just living in the moment.

Clearly, I had taken a turn from my first marriage and was going in the opposite direction of living a worry-free life loaded with spontaneity. It was fun, and it was perfect.

On good days, Mark was the charming life of the party, very generous and up for anything. One day, early in our relationship, he suggested we jump into his van and drive to Winslow, Arizona.

Loading a cooler with sandwiches, beer, and a sipper bottle of something, probably tequila, we headed out. Turning up the tunes, our toes were tapping, and we were singing along to Jethro Tull, The Allman Brothers, Leon Russell, and other classic rock groups as we pointed the van south for a 700-mile road trip.

It was raining heavily when we arrived in Winslow. Slowly driving around, exploring the town, our sightseeing was somewhat limited through the overworked wiper blades smacking the rain off the windshield. We cruised down a fairly deserted, central main street when the colorful striped awning over a local store front beckoned to us.

Laughing hysterically, we hopped out of the van to hustle over to stand under the awning. There, we had done it—we were standing in the rain on the corner, watching a three-dimensional theater unfold all around us in Winslow, Arizona.

Older model, well-used farm pickups, often with a grizzled, hat-wearing farmer or cowboy at the wheel, were the most common mode of transportation. A few people hurried down the sidewalk, moving quickly while hugging the sides of the buildings to avoid the direct, steady rain.

A well-dressed, late-sixtyish woman exited the shop from the door behind us, a pocketbook resting on her slightly raised right arm. Distracted, she moved only a few steps in the dry area under the awning, adjusting her raincoat and umbrella. She was startled when she looked up and noticed us for the first time.

Nobody said anything as she turned slightly to direct an unabashed look at us—up and down, most pointedly at Mark. She was taking in his hair, grown past his shoulders, the tinted glasses he was wearing in defiance of the rain, his favorite, ancient blue jeans, and a well-worn denim shirt I had hand-embroidered for him. Glancing at the rain, she turned, her attention mostly on Mark as she uttered a slight, but ladylike, snuffle, "Don't worry, hippie. There's no soap in it."

Adjusting her collar, she extended her hand beyond the awning edge to capture a few drops of rain, and with a final, slight backward glance, she stepped into the rain shower and walked briskly up the street.

We watched in silence as she walked away. Neither of us said a word as we turned, looked at each other, and burst out laughing.

That was all we needed to conclude that adventure. Giddy from that brief exchange, we raced through the rain to the van for the drive home.

So yes, on a good day Mark was spontaneous with a unique sense of humor. He enjoyed a great deal of fun by means of his huge passion for life.

However, because of his high level of intelligence, he also had his version of how things should go. "Perfection," "doing things his way," "this is not for discussion" were also his world. With his lofty version of faultlessness, he easily became impatient. People, pets, traffic, standing in lines, children, older people, weather, equipment—the list was extensive, and all these variables often very easily frustrated him. He began taking those frustrations out on me.

At first, his subtle verbal jabs caught me off guard. The more successful he became in his professional life, the more he verbally poked and demeaned me.

A noticeable shift first occurred during a normal after work conversation, and this was the first time his words really stung. At this point, his business was thriving, and my own job responsibilities revolved around managing an airline human resources staff of seven. We were both home from work and just hanging out, catching up on chatter while puttering around in the kitchen preparing dinner. During the easy banter, I mentioned a simple work matter, asking his opinion how he would handle something like that.

As rapidly as someone flipping a switch, the civil conversation reverted to him yelling at me! He flew off the handle, telling me how he did not respect anyone who had to work for somebody else. "You people are losers!" he yelled. He "only respected people who built something successful from scratch. If a person can't figure out how to be successful as their own boss in their own business, then working for somebody else who doesn't have time for them, blah, blah, blah ..."

Just as abruptly as he would blow up, he would stop the bullying. I was stunned and backpedaled to change the subject, sputtering, "Jeez, I was just curious how you would handle something ..." Interrupting me again, he shouted, "Well, if you are that fucking stupid, why do they have you running the department?"

Ding, ding—that concluded SmackDown, Round 1, and I didn't even know a fight was scheduled.

Our priorities evolved from happily scraping together beer money, to rubbing elbows with presidents and CEO's at local, national, and international business functions.

Attending these often-formal affairs, my instructions were given prior to entering the restaurant or party venue. First was a reminder that he did not see where I needed to speak to or speak with anyone there. "You'll just embarrass yourself and me." He often followed this up with, "Just be quiet because nobody wants to hear what you have to say. Just keep your fucking mouth shut so you don't sound stupid." Or his go-to, "Goddamn it, Shari," forcefully spoken at the start and/or finish of most sentences directed my way.

Yes, he was very direct.

Wow, what happened? I was conflicted with this new behavior and rationalized, *He's my husband, whom I love and respect. Therefore, this must be just a phase; he had a difficult day; something must've gone sideways at work; he's tired; he's hung over; I must've done-said-implied something wrong.*

Whatever the excuse du jour, I numbly accepted his verbal goading and his strong suggestion that I was nowhere near him in the brains department where, he repeatedly told me, he, his employees, and his business contacts resided. I would sadly conclude this self-talk with, *Therefore, he must be right.*

My "high verbal" personality was completely smacked down, so I took his cue and defeatedly assumed my role of keeping quiet. To cope, my go-to prop accelerated to keeping a full adult beverage in my hand at all times. I realized that when I was holding a glass, sipping, nodding, and smiling, I was doing exactly as he ordered and not talking. I convinced myself that if I was relegated to silence, this beverage may as well take the edge off the ache I felt in my heart.

Even though the majority in our wide circle of friends and business contacts saw us in a healthy, fun relationship, a few close friends witnessed his rapidly increasing amount of verbal abuse. It had become uncomfortable for not only me but for those who were witness to this shift.

Driving home from work the Friday before a long Fourth of July weekend, I was lost in thought, anticipating the big, fun, party filled three-day weekend with friends we planned to host. As I was turning at a stoplight, a young man ran the light, T-boning and demolishing the front of my car. It was a mess, with the front smashed in nearly to the dashboard. The radiator, what was left of it, was steaming, and fluids were gushing onto the pavement from under the wreckage. Those other drivers involved were shaken up, although luckily, no one seemed injured. Several passersby stopped to help push my car to the side of the road.

Hearing the crash, people ran out of nearby houses to help, advising they already notified police. Was there anyone else they could call for me? Again, this was prior to cell phones. Shaken up by the accident, I was very grateful for their concern and asked if I could use their phone to call my husband.

Walking away from the wreck toward their nearby house, we heard a *crash*. Another driver was distracted looking at the wreck and ran into the back of my car. Not only was my car front end smashed, the trunk was smashed in so badly my car looked like an accordion—it was totaled.

Badly shaken, I made the call to Mark, explaining the accident. His first words back to me were, "Well, you really know how to fuck up my weekend, don't you?"

He never asked if I was all right; what, if any, damage there was to the car; or if anybody else was hurt. He was clearly irritated that he had to stop whatever he was doing to drive the one and a half miles to the scene to get me.

Yes, it was a time when I felt very small, useless, and utterly stupid. There was a clear shift in me from a carefree and happy "me," to not liking, or even recognizing, this disconnected and lost part of "me"—the part of me who felt too stupid to exist was beginning to feel unsafe around him—yet, I continued to do what I was told.

In my case, as the recipient of verbal abuse, I often felt I had done something to deserve it—and that was exactly the rabbit hole I was going down. Constantly rationalizing Mark's behaviors in my head, I had convinced myself whatever I'd done or whatever happened to make his day bad, it would soon blow over. The next minute, next hour, or next day, he was just fine, acting like nothing happened, or as I thought, *Being his usual self.* Followed up with, *See? You are right. No big deal. Just a phase, not really him.*

His abusive behavior escalated, causing me to withdraw even further into myself. I began to find myself often apologizing, and "I'm sorry" became my automatic response to him and to anybody who may have overheard him, the clerk he barked at in the store, or ... you get the picture. Even though I felt myself shrinking, I remained determined to stand by him and see him through "this phase."

RECREATIONAL DRUGS were often in the picture—after all, how did one party all day and all night, get up, and work a full day and do it all again without Momma's little helpers?

Recognizing Mark's behaviors were becoming a problem and may be escalating to threatening, I retreated even further by upping the self-medication to deaden my pain. Most days, it was easier for me to simply check out. I just numbly watched all this crazy stuff go on around me; this made it far less complicated to deal with him or the situation, and it was easy for me to do.

In order for me to manage the stress, heartache, and confusion of this problematic time in my life and marriage, I naively reinforced my resolve to simply block it out of my thinking. We all know that when we want to just not think about something, that "something" becomes all you think about.

Around this time, I did find another method to help clear my mind—weekly meditation classes at the home of my friend Sandi. Sandi's classes allowed me the nonjudgmental space to stumble through my life issues. Oftentimes, I found slivers of peace as I worked to sort out my life and my most often used and easiest remedy, self-medication with unhealthy amounts of alcohol and pharmaceuticals.

Professionally, I was then working with a large, local travel management company that handled several significant local and national accounts. One account was managing the travel incentive program for a large insurance holding company that owned many of the well-known life insurance companies of that era. The travel assignments related to this account offered me much-needed relief away from my volatile home environment.

The insurance holding company promoted a variety of sales incentives, including top tier travel packages awarded to their highest producing agents, plus a guest. Our agency was tasked with creating, organizing, and conducting these trips to exclusive resorts on the mainland US, Hawaii, the Caribbean, and other international destinations.

One of my responsibilities was escorting and traveling with these groups. Our team would arrive at the destination a day or two prior to the guests' arrival to ensure amenities, transportation, food, speakers, and recreational programs were in place.

At the start of the program, we would meet and greet the guests as they arrived, run the daily work and recreational programs, and organize the tours, the meals, and any add-on functions the client selected. At the conclusion, our team ensured the guests were checked out of the location and safely on their way home. The remaining members of our team would wrap up final details with the hotel, and once everything was buttoned down, we would head back to home base.

The entire travel team worked long hours and many days directly with the guests, as well as managing the project from behind the scenes. The trade-off to these long days and hard work was that it took us to some of the most beautiful resort locations in the world.

As Mother-Vic proudly shared with her friends, "My daughter is a paid escort—she travels all over the world, taking care of executives."

The first time I heard her explanation and saw the look on the other person's face as they gave me an eyebrow-raised sideways glance? "Whoa. Whoa. Whoooooooa—all true, but please, let me explain!"

Chapter Eight

ON FEBRUARY 21, 1989, our small meditation group of a dozen or so people met as usual at Sandi's house for our class and time together. My plan was to attend this class, then depart two days later for my next work assignment, a week in Australia escorting one of the large insurance client groups.

This Australia trip involved moving several hundred guests from all points in the US to Sydney, then moving the entire group to functions at a variety of other Australian destinations. This was our agency's first trip to Australia, so I was scheduled to arrive a couple of days early to adjust for jet lag and to get organized. The total trip was nine days.

Leaving class that evening, Sandi asked me to stay behind to speak with me about the trip. She shared a premonition and her concern that I would experience a stress-filled trip and I would be very happy to return home.

Taken aback as she shared her thoughts, I wondered, *Whoa, is she ever off base on this one. No way will I be stressed. This trip will be fun—I am excited by a new adventure, looking forward to time away from my difficult home situation. Plus, who wouldn't love time in Australia! She's wrong.*

As we concluded our conversation, she did not budge as she stood, looking me straight in the eye. Reaching out to me, she drew me to her for a long, warm hug. Nobody in our class ever hugged Sandi, nor had seen her hug any other person. As a teacher, she felt hugging students was ill-suited for her detached teaching style, and we all respected that.

Those of our group who remained with me after class gasped as well because close personal contact was completely out of character for her. All this information and hugging was totally unexpected, and it rattled me. In time, I would recognize that Sandi had once again displayed her uncanny accuracy. She was right; my journey began to spiral into one of the most difficult and stress-filled times in my life.

THE MORNING OF February 23, 1989, dawned and Rita, my longtime Denver friend, surprised me by showing up at the airline departure gate. Remember, this was long before airport security, cell phones, and the internet.

Rita and I met in the early '70s when I interviewed for my first Denver airline job with a startup regional carrier, Pioneer Airlines.

While nervously waiting in the airline's office lobby for my interview with the manager, I looked up from the outdated, dog-eared magazine I'd been flipping through to realize this woman was speaking to me in a brisk New York accent. She needed a ride from the office to a meeting across the street at the airport. So, when was I leaving?

Struggling to keep up with the rapid-fire conversation with this petite, no-nonsense, smart, savvy, hilariously funny, native New Yorker, I learned she worked in a customer service management position at Pioneer, and let's say, she was and remains "very direct" in how she conducts her personal and professional life.

Immediately switching gears in my head from reading a boring magazine article to plugging into this New York-style conversation with a total stranger, I explained I was there for an interview and unsure of my schedule. No matter, she made a plan for me to drop her at the terminal after my interview.

That day all worked in my favor. I was able to drive Rita to her meeting and also accepted an administrative position working closely with Rita, along with a number of other managers there who have remained my good friends.

Even with our widely different rural Iowa and New

York City environments, Rita and I discovered much common ground that revolved around our comparable, close-knit family lives. We were both raised by WWII Marine fathers who married solid and humorous women. We also both enjoyed time with our large, extended families, plus her New York neighborhood experiences growing up and my Iowa small-town life experiences were surprisingly alike, although in what could not possibly be more opposite settings. That was the beginning of our very long and enduring friendship.

On my departure day for Australia, Rita's surprise appearance at the gate was significant because meeting or taking someone all the way to the gate was not the usual drop off or pick up routine for frequently traveling airline folks.

Normally, we simply dropped someone at the curb, so I had to ask, "What are you doing here?"

"I'm here to talk you out of flying on this itinerary. I am going to arrange a ticket for you on (another airline)."

We both recognized the United gate agent and included her in the conversation. The three of us discussed switching carriers, concluding that since all the current arrangements were set, my bags were checked, and the flight was departing soon, it made no sense to create a great deal of drama by switching carriers.

Rita left it at, "Well, be sure you have a safe trip."

Um, what? That "have a safe trip" comment was also

out of character and the equivalent of me driving to the nearest grocery store but first being walked to the car by a family member and told to "have a safe trip."

After the incident, I asked Rita about that comment. She admitted she had a "funny feeling" and was compelled to meet up with me to convince me to change airlines. When the itinerary did not change, she simply said what she was thinking. Weird.

MY FLIGHT ITINERARY WAS Denver—Los Angeles—Honolulu—Auckland—Sydney. Looking back, another unusual event occurred when my flight landed in Los Angeles. The long connecting time to my Honolulu flight allowed me the opportunity to locate a pay phone and call Cindy, Mark's sister in Tulsa. As much as I traveled with my job and for personal reasons, and as much as Cindy traveled, calling her on a trip simply to check in was also clearly out of the ordinary.

Cindy and her younger brother exhibited similar dynamic personalities as she, too, lived her life with a great passion. Any time spent with this funny, generous, bighearted character was always chaotic and fun. When we spoke, she mentioned how happy she was that I had called because she was just thinking about me and wanted to wish me fun travels and to "be safe."

Whoa, another moment of pause for me. This was turning into a very unusual conversation between us because getting on and off airplanes was not a "big event" for either us. Laughing as I regained my composure, I replied, "What? I'm just going to Australia to work for a week—what could possibly go wrong?"

Landing and deplaning in Honolulu, it felt good to stretch and walk around prior to checking in for the flight to Auckland. Due to my travel industry employee status, the Honolulu United gate agent offered a professional courtesy and upgraded me from my originally assigned seat 40C in coach to seat 9F in business class.

The United agents at gate ten boarded the regular passengers first, then checking passenger loads, they determined what seats were still available. They assigned those empty seats to standby airline and travel industry employees. By the time the agent completed the procedures and issued my upgraded boarding pass, I was one of the final passengers to board for Auckland.

Scurrying down the jetway, boarding pass in hand, I marched across the aircraft threshold to enter the eighteen-year-old Boeing 747. Pausing slightly before stepping onto the aircraft's well-worn flooring, I couldn't help but notice the paint-chipped door track and door locking mechanisms. Chuckling quietly, I thought, "Wow, this is an old airplane. I sure hope it makes it across the Pacific."

I hastily made my way toward my seat—9F in the business class section, counting the seats as I went. Reaching 9F, a well-dressed, executive-level gentleman had already occupied the seat. He was settled in, drink in hand, and quietly chatting with the passenger on his left.

I politely interrupted his conversation with his seat-mate, "I'm sorry, it appears you are in my seat. I'm seated in 9F."

Turning, he looked over his right shoulder at me, and before he said one word, I could see by the expression on his face that the idea of him moving or any potential seating inconvenience annoyed him. Irritated, he pulled his boarding pass from the seat pocket in front of him and sure enough—he, too, was holding seat 9F.

Clearly a duplicate seating mix-up happened in the gate agent's final rush to complete the boarding process.

This passenger was firm and clear that he was already settled in, and I did not blame him for not being interested in packing up to move to another seat. With that, he returned his attention to his seat companion.

A flight attendant stepped over to investigate why I had not taken my seat and realized it was a simple seating matter.

Duplicate seating assignments are easily corrected and having to take another seat did not phase me at all. As a travel industry employee, being upgraded was a courtesy, and we were trained to cheerfully accept any hiccups that could possibly affect a paying passenger. I was not flying as a full fare-paying passenger, so industry protocol required me "to go with the flow." For any travel employee, their family member or one of their buddy pass fliers/friends to ever create an issue or scene while traveling on standby? That could cost the employee their job. Yes, airline management was that serious about keeping industry travel hassle-free, especially for full-fare revenue passengers.

The flight attendant hastily advised me they needed to conclude boarding, close the doors, and push back. The aircraft couldn't move without everybody seated and buckled in and with a sweep of her hand, she motioned and briskly instructed me to "sit anywhere."

Turning to scan my empty seat options, I plopped down into the first available seat, 13F, the last row of business class. The bulkhead and galley were located directly behind me and I was four rows behind my originally assigned 9F seat.

Now seated and hastily buckled in 13F, I took a deep breath and looked around the business class cabin, curious and intrigued about those sitting around me. It seemed as though time slowed as I took an extra moment to really notice my fellow travelers. My thoughts turned to *that was weird* as I wondered why I felt compelled to really "see" everyone.

Chapter Nine

UNITED 811, DEPARTING HONOLULU, HAWAII
FEBRUARY 24, 1989

UNITED FLIGHT 811 DEPARTED HONOLULU International Airport February 24, 1989, at 1:52 a.m. local time,
carrying 337 passengers and eighteen crew members.

This flight was manned with an experienced flight
crew consisting of thirty-five-year veteran Captain David
Cronin, who was just months shy of the then-mandatory
retirement age of sixty. Also on the flight deck were First
Officer Greg Slater (age forty-eight) and Second Officer
Randall "Mark" Thomas (age forty-six). Most of the
cabin crew were senior staff in their thirties and forties
and had flown for a number of years.

After taking off from Honolulu, Captain Cronin

decided to detour around the thunderstorms that were building in the area, which meant he was "hands on" flying the aircraft. He anticipated some weather-related turbulence and left the seat belt sign on, in what turned out to be a lifesaving decision for many passengers that night.

Filling the cabin was the usual muffled hum of the engines. The flight crew prepared the cabin for their first service, and passengers made themselves comfortable for the remainder of the flight.

Whether the seat belt sign is on or off, my personal preference has always been to only loosen my seat belt, never unbuckling it unless I need to move about the cabin.

Watching the familiar crew ritual and listening to the muted chatter in the galley behind me, I loosened my seat belt, located my book, and considered taking a sedative to allow me to sleep the entire eight-hour flight to Auckland.

Still absentmindedly observing the other passengers settling in and starting to relax, a thought popped into my head. *No, don't take anything. You may need your wits about you, in case there is an emergency.*

Spending as much time as I did in my own head, this cautionary thought was not normal thinking, even for me—and especially not for an airline employee and frequent traveler.

It startled me because that was not a thought or feeling I'd ever had while flying, and it unnerved me. Sitting stunned for a few more seconds, I wondered what that was about, then tried to shake it off by picking up my book to begin reading.

Reading quietly, and only minutes later, a young man loudly whispered in my right ear, "Tighten your seat belt. You're in for the ride of your life."

My head snapped up at that odd instruction. "Huh? What?" For all I knew, it was a flight attendant who leaned around the bulkhead.

Quickly turning in my seat, attempting to discover the origin of that unusual directive, I wondered what crew member ever gave such an instruction to an individual passenger. It made no sense.

Nobody was standing there. Not a soul was moving anywhere up or down the aisle.

From my seat, looking all the way to the back of the aircraft, not one person was up or moving. We were still climbing out and flying around the thunderstorm. The seat belt sign remained lit.

Having worked for three airlines and in the travel industry for many years, no flight crew member was trained to, nor would they ever give, that type of command. Plus, it sounded prophetic, and in my gut, I realized something extraordinary had just happened.

My heart raced, and seconds passed as I gathered myself, thinking, *That was just too weird. I am going to give this seat belt an extra tug.*

Feeling anxious, I gave my seat belt a couple of

additional yanks to ensure it was snug. Nervously placing the book in my lap and tipping my seat back, I stuck
my thumbs into the seat belt like a cowboy gunslinger
hooking into his gun belt.

With my eyes closed, sighing and taking several deep
breaths to gather my thoughts, I willed myself to concen-
trate on regulating my rapid breathing and racing heart.

We'd only been in the air less than ten minutes since
takeoff and were steadily climbing out of Honolulu. We
did experience a few small bumps as we passed from
22,000 feet to 23,000 feet on our way to 33,000 feet,
but those bumps were no big deal. We were a little over
four miles above the Pacific Ocean.

An unusual grinding noise suddenly emanated from
beneath my feet—a sound I had never heard on an airborne aircraft. Alarmed, my eyes flew open; every fiber
of my being warned me . . . *That did not sound right.*
That was not right.

The airplane began to shake and vibrate in a significant and unnatural manner.

What we did not know then was that the right-side
forward cargo door was experiencing an electrical malfunction, causing it to slowly unlatch from the normal
locked and secured position. The flight crew later reported they were shown no warning indicator lights flashing
in the cockpit, signaling this soon to be catastrophic malfunction.

In just seconds, we experienced the grinding noise.

Then, a brief one and a half seconds later, there was a loud thump and jolt—similar to hitting an unexpected pothole.

The thump was even more ominous sounding. From the weather-related bumpy ride, to the grinding noise followed by considerable vibration, to the loud bump? In that moment, the thump was the opening in the aircraft cargo door seal, which mildly depressurized the aircraft cargo area. Instantly, the slightly open right-side forward gull-like cargo door was caught in the wind and ripped violently upwards.

ACTUAL BLACK BOX TRANSCRIPT

Codes are:

Capt-Captain

FO-First Officer

Und-Undetermined

Tower-Control Tower

Eng-Engineer

CAPT—WHAT THE #### WAS THAT?

FO—I DON'T KNOW

Und—THE ENGINE

FO—OKAY, AH, IT LOOKS LIKE WE'VE LOST NUMBER THREE ENGINE

FO—AND, AH, WE'RE DESCENDING RAPIDLY COMING BACK

TOWER—UNITED EIGHT ELEVEN HEAVY ROGER KEEP CENTER ADVISED

CAPT—CALL THE (AFT) FLIGHT ATTENDANT

The immediate explosion and damage created when the cargo door ripped up and away from the aircraft triggered a rapid decompression, which burst open the fuselage.

This catastrophic event caused the aircraft's floor on the right side of the fuselage to cave in beneath seats 8G/H through 12G/H.

Ten total seats, eight seats with passengers, were instantly pulled into the dark night over the Pacific Ocean.

An empty seat, a flapping seat belt, and a bent armrest showed the fate of the ninth passenger fatality—the gentleman seated in 9F, my originally assigned seat.

Those nine people disappeared into the night in the blink of an eye.

While reading this, you blinked. Think about that. Look at something—blink—and it's gone. That is how fast it happened that nine people around me perished. Just. Like. That.

My first thoughts were total disbelief, *This is a United Airlines 747. This cannot be happening.* Then the realization, *Well, this is happening.*

There was no compartment in my brain to place what we were experiencing.

The explosion produced a huge, gaping hole, large enough to drive a truck through, and it was on the right side of me.

Shocked, I stared down through that tattered and shorn hole in the fuselage onto scattered clouds, and beneath those clouds to an unobstructed ocean view. Those

THE VIEW FROM 13F

seats, the floor, and passengers that were there? All gone.

So significant was the decompression at that altitude, the loss of cabin pressure created a deafening, catastrophic, hurricane force wind, and everything near the explosion that was not buckled in had become a dangerous, flying projectile.

The decompression demolished the business class section. Flying cabin debris, aircraft panels, oxygen masks, wiring, carry-on baggage, service items, and carts all initially rushed past, battering those of us seated near the damage.

Much of the aircraft's interior was sucked out the gaping hole and into the darkness of the night. Ripped and torn wires, now exposed, were hanging down, and the cabin was suddenly filled with debris and fog.

Fighting to breathe with the 350-mph incoming cold wind, I searched for an oxygen mask. It was clear from the stripped bare walls and ceiling above us, there were none. The oxygen masks were gone. They, too, were part of the debris scattered across the Pacific. Even if they had deployed, there was no oxygen available as the emergency oxygen lines were damaged when the cargo door separated from the fuselage.

CAPT—I CAN'T GET ANY OXYGEN
FO—(DID WE AH)
FO—YOU OKAY?
CAPT—YEAH
FO—ARE YOU GETTIN' OXYGEN?

FO—WE'RE NOT GETTIN' ANY OXYGEN

In the darkness of the heavily damaged aircraft, the cabin crew made attempts to gather themselves. People were injured, and at 24,000 feet, the air temperature was approximately twenty degrees below with the wind rushing back in through that hole at a gale force.

Captain Cronin immediately descended to 15,000 feet to stabilize the aircraft and also in search of breathable air.

The extreme vibrations wildly rocked the dark and damaged aircraft; it felt like it would soon break apart in midair. To my right, those two engines had burst into fireballs after taking in most of the cabin debris. Of the two engines, engine three ingested the bulk of what flew out of the aircraft and was immediately shut down, due to the intense vibrations.

FO—I THINK WE BLEW A DOOR. THINK WE BLEW A . . . OR SOMTHIN'

CAPT—OKAY WE LOST NUMBER AH THREE

CAPT—LET'S AH SHUT IT DOWN

FO—YEAH OKAY

FO—READY FOR NUMBER THREE

FO—SHUTDOWN CHECKLIST

The engines' flames to my right were directly in my line of sight. The incoming wind and the earsplitting, high-pitched whine of the battered 747 engines were deafening. The damaged and wildly flailing wires that had been torn out of the aircraft ceiling were hanging there, jiggling in the wind. All around the cabin, every time the loose wires moved against each other, they burst into eerie sparks. For all I knew, each electrical spark was another trigger for a bomb, and this time we might completely blow up.

The passengers on my left—a man, his pregnant wife, and their six-year-old daughter sitting between them, were comforting each other. The father placed a small airline pillow over the child's face and later shared that they covered her face with the pillow not only for protection. They did not want her to see what we all knew was inevitable.

Unable to communicate due to the intense noise, I leaned to my left and instinctively wrapped my arms around the right leg of the father. He acted as my anchor, so I would not be pulled out of the gaping hole. Hanging on to him with all my strength, I did not know if there would be more aircraft breaking off. My thoughts rapidly turned to considering potential catastrophes: *Would we be sucked out? Would more of the floor collapse under us? Would we all be blown out? Or blown apart at the next spark? Am I hanging on until we crash into the sea?*

After holding on for one or two minutes, I gingerly released the father's leg and sat up to look around. I couldn't believe what I saw. I was even more horrified as the realization of the seriousness of our situation hit me. Turning back to reattach myself to his leg, I squeezed my eyes closed and waited for the next explosion—and our certain death.

After a minute, I sat up for the second time. Turning to my right, it was apparent the two passengers across the aisle from me, also in row thirteen, were in grave danger, bouncing around in their broken and unstable seats.

Both passengers were clearly in shock, and the wife in the window seat, her head was bloodied from debris that had forcibly blew past them at the moment of the explosive decompression.

Because the floor holding the seats in rows eight through twelve had been ripped out, the floor area in front of the two passengers in row thirteen suffered significant damage. There was little flooring in front of them, and their feet were hanging out the hole while their broken, unstable seats were pitched forward at an additional thirty-degree angle, no longer completely secured to the floor.

Releasing my hold on the father to my left and leaning across the aisle, I grabbed and held row thirteen husband's left arm. His left hand was gripping his armrest, so using one, then two hands, I squeezed and held his left arm in an effort to hold him in his seat.

Over the commotion, I motioned frantically, working to distract him and his bloodied, dazed wife to look away from the hole. The loud engines, wind, and noise made it impossible to speak, so I continued to hold on and implored them, through hand motions, to look at me rather than what was ahead of them.

His wife remained motionless, looking straight ahead

across the expanse of missing seats and floor, numbly staring at the flight attendant belted into his jump seat, seated facing back at her. Had the seats and passengers still been in place, she could not have seen him.

My frantic and only thought while holding that passenger's arm was, *At what point do I let go of him? Am I going to be able to hold him in this seat when it breaks off? I can't let go of him, but will holding on pull me out with him?* I was certain that at the next explosion or hard shudder they would be next to be sucked out of the hole into the black night.

While the cabin crew frantically assessed the chaotic situation, passengers were holding each other, looking around, helpless. Surprisingly, the passengers in my line of sight appeared stunned and in shock, while also taking in the scene. Clearly, there were seats and people missing—seats and people that were right there just minutes ago.

What the hell just happened here? was all I could process because what I witnessed was simply surreal.

The explosive decompression pulled a flight attendant out of the galley behind me, and she was stuck under the seats of the two passengers on my right. She was terribly contorted, dazed, and she was injured.

She appeared to be twisted in a way that made it impossible to dislodge herself or even move. In a panic, she looked at me with a what's-going-on expression. Releasing my hold on the row thirteen passenger's arm,

I reached over to her. Holding her hand with my right hand, with my left hand, I attempted to point out the damage and demonstrate what happened. With hand motions as our only form of communication, I hoped I was getting through to her, considering the circumstances. She was able to reach up and pull a seat back cushion out of the seat to protectively place over her head. She remained there, curled up on the floor, until another flight attendant battled the strong, incoming wind to work her way over to assist.

Talking was simply impossible over the incredible noise from the high pitch whine of the engines, the engine fire, and the incoming wind.

There was no mistaking this was not going to end well.

We were on fire, critically damaged, and we were falling out of the sky.

Chapter Ten

ONE HUNDRED MILES FROM HAWAII, SOMEWHERE OVER THE PACIFIC OCEAN EARLY MORNING, FEBRUARY 24, 1989

THE UNITED 811 FLIGHT CREW, while highly experienced and well trained in handling many catastrophic events, realized their cockpit procedures manual did not have a game plan for the magnitude of challenges during this incident. They were literally flying by the seat of their pants.

The crew fought to keep us in the air. There was the gaping hole, which had damaged the fuselage, the unknown additional structural damage, and the fires in engines three and four which required engine shut down.

The aircraft carried a full load of fuel, passengers, and

luggage/cargo. There was likely significant, undiscovered systems damage. With all that, the crew remained uncertain of what had even happened as they struggled to maintain altitude.

A flight attendant positioned at the front of the cabin in the left aisle struggled to demonstrate and secure her own life vest—a difficult task considering the strength of the incoming wind. As she secured the vest, she began screaming instructions though a megaphone, the veins on her neck standing out as she desperately tried to communicate with passengers and other crew members—yet, with all the confusion and noise, we heard nothing.

Those passengers paying attention to the flight crew were relieved to have a crew member somewhat in charge and offering instructions. To this point, passengers could only sit, helpless in their seats, as the aircraft broke apart around them. Doing something, anything, felt good, and there was some small action we could take to help ourselves.

Reaching under my seat to locate and retrieve the bagged vest, I realized that where I sat, facing directly into the freezing, gale force wind, there were no do-overs should the life vest be blown or ripped out of my hands. This was my only chance to put on this potentially life-saving vest before …

Stop right there ordered my internal voice, as I forced myself not to go that direction in my thinking.

I knew that in order to successfully don the vest, I

must slow down my thoughts, turn things way down, several notches down, to super deliberate actions.

Slowly reaching under my seat to grip the vest storage bag with both hands, I painstakingly brought it up to my lap. Cautiously opening the bag to expose the life vest and carefully tucking the then-useless storage bag trash into the seat back, I clutched the vest with both of my numb and stiffening hands. Trembling from fear and cold, I tried to take another deep breath before unfolding the vest.

Determinedly fighting against that freezing, swirling wind, I slowly positioned the vest to place over my head and then felt enormous relief after successfully pulling the vest down to my shoulders and securing the clasps, and pulling the inflation tab.

Everyone around me stayed seated—where were they going to go and what were they going to do at 14,000 feet? People traveling together, or perhaps even strangers, held each other. Many likely shared what they believed to be their final words.

Then we waited in the dark and bitter incoming wind. Our only light sources were the bright moonlight coming in through the hole, or through the aircraft windows, or from the brief flashes of sparks when the broken wires touched together.

We could only watch the other passengers and the flight crews' handle challenges created by the aircraft's instability as we pitched downward, toward the ocean.

Stepping outside of my head for a moment, I looked out at the clouds below. The reflection from the bright moon turned the scattered fluffy clouds a beautiful shade of gray with a shining silver sheen outline that reflected off the Pacific Ocean. My brain paused on, *Geez, if this wasn't so scary, that would really be beautiful.*

My thoughts turned to what it is you think about when you know you are going to die.

Time slowed as I began pondering that age-old question. A strange out-of-body stillness and calm came over me, even as all the noise, engine fire, and chaos raged around me throughout the cabin.

Wow. So this is how I'm going to die. Who knew? I wonder if I will drown? Ugh, the water will be so cold. Crap, when we hit, there will be oil, fuel, pieces of the crash. Body parts—will that draw sharks? Will it be a shark attack? That'll be nasty to drown in oily, smelly water. We'll probably just break up in air and fall out of the sky. Whoa, what would that feel like—to free fall for miles? I am so cold . . .

They'll prepare us to ditch, but when we hit the water, we'll break up. Might as well crash on the runway, same result. Wonder if I'll get tangled up in the cabin debris; will I drown before I get out? Or I won't get out and sink with the airplane? . . .

You get the picture.

In the midst of these surreal and terrifying circumstances, my thoughts were surprisingly matter of fact.

An out-of-body sensation overtook me, as though I were viewing and critiquing the situation, rather than experiencing it.

Detached and observing all that was happening around me, it was clear this event would not be survivable. There were no options; it was time for me to face the inevitable.

My heart ached with the realization that I was desperately alone in my last moments, and my thoughts drifted to my life up to this point.

Wow. Only minutes into this routine flight, and then just like that, I reached the end of my Earthly days? Boy, that was quick.

At thirty-seven years old, my life was over already? How quickly a routine day can change and rearrange everything. I boarded an airplane for a business trip, and now I was going to die. Was anything left unsaid with anybody? If so, I realized that would be my biggest regret.

Unable to identify one single regret on anything I had ever done, I realized any possible regrets were for anything I had left undone—actions I did not take, times I chose to not participate or held back for whatever reason, including those times I listened to another person rather than listening to my own best self.

Not one thing in my head turned to or had awareness of anything related to material matters.

For the first time, I fully stepped out of my head and clearly felt what was in my heart.

Never for one second was it, *Damn it. I wish I would have worked longer, harder, made more money, had a bigger house, a faster car.*

All my thoughts and concerns were solely focused on experiences and relationships, the quality of those relationships, my part in those relationships, and the quality of my life.

Thoughts of my family were foremost in my mind. My heart ached with an unmistakable, visceral sense of profound sadness for their impending grief.

I wondered how they would cope when they learned the news of this event and I reflected on how upset they would be as they replayed in their minds their projected version of my final moments.

Perhaps they would believe that I was terrified—even horrified, or in pain, or scared. The truth was these final moments were all that, and even more. But I also knew I would be OK with however this flight terminated. And that was a great comfort to me.

Still, I was feeling sad because how could my family and friends ever understand this peaceful surrender?

This final experience was as real as it gets. There was no fight in me; there was no place to hide or resist what was about to happen. My only choice was to simply and completely give myself up to this experience.

Plus, I felt an overwhelming sense that I was surrounded by "something" and not alone—that, in my final moment, I would be taken care of in a way I could not Earthly comprehend, I could only experience.

With a heavy heart, I felt my loved ones would probably carry their own distress, not knowing I was fine and in those final moments, there was no fear. My only thoughts were good thoughts of them, which also comforted me. I would leave this world feeling content and satisfied with my brief, Earthly time with them. They were with me in my mind, and that brought me great emotional comfort and tranquility.

On the other hand, my thoughts were also of them carrying their own anguish, grief, and sorrow until we would meet again, wondering if they would waste time grieving, rather than celebrating me, my life, and what we enjoyed together.

In that instant, it became so clear to me that when we are gone, the best thing our loved ones can do is to celebrate us, not mourn us!

With a sad smile, certain these were my final moments, this revelation was gut-wrenching. But one thing I knew for sure: my family and friends knew how to celebrate and have a good time. I just hoped they would joyfully celebrate what we each had together, and in some way, my legacy would motivate them to go on to create their own best lives.

Thoughts regarding my husband? That was difficult, and my feelings were torn. However, deep down, and upon much reflection later, I knew this was the part of me that died that day.

With the conclusion and finality of that mental exercise, there was no doubt my feelings were clear.

Awaiting my fate, I was at peace. I was focused on my final minutes and now curious about how this was going to go, wondering what exactly happens the moment my life is over. Taking a deep breath, I was convinced I was about to find out.

Turning my head to look straight into the wind and out the hole into the dark night, it was clear this was my last great, Earthly adventure. We could not stay airborne much longer as we continued our bumpy downwards ride toward the ocean.

The flight deck was unable to reach the flight attendants on the damaged intercom system. Captain Cronin sent Second Officer Thomas down the stairs from the upper floor cockpit to investigate. Officer Thomas descended the stairs, and I watched as he stopped to take his first look at the chaos in the cabin. Even in the darkness, his face displayed the shock and seriousness of the situation as he quickly took in the sight of the gaping hole, the damage, the missing floor and seats, and the apparent fire in engine four. It looked like a bomb had gone off.

Second Officer Thomas quickly turned and raced up the stairs to report and get back to work in the cockpit.

FO—YOU GOT A FIRE OUT THERE

CAPT—THERE'S A FIRE OUT THERE?

FO—YEAH LOOKS LIKE IT'S ENGINE NUMBER FOUR

CAPT—WHICH ONE
FO—LOOKS LIKE NUMBER—NUMBER FOUR
HOLD ON A SECOND—
CAPT—YEAH WE GOT A FIRE IN NUMBER
FOUR
CAPT—GO THROUGH THE PROCEDURE
SHUT DOWN THE ENGINE

Seeing the cockpit crew member meant the cockpit did not separate from the aircraft, as it did in the Lockerbie disaster. The crew was alive, and they had control of the aircraft.

ENG—THE WHOLE RIGHT SIDE . . .
ENG—THE RIGHT SIDE IS GONE FROM
ABOUT THE AH ONE RIGHT BACK IT'S JUST
OPEN YOU'RE JUST LOOKIN' OUTSIDE
TOWER—UNITED EIGHT ELEVEN HEAVY
ROGER
CAPT—WADDAYA MEAN PIECES
ENG—LOOKS LIKE A BOMB
FO—FUSELAGE
ENG—YES FUSELAGE IT'S JUST OPEN
CAPT—OKAY IT LOOKS LIKE WE GOT A
BOMB AH THAT WENT OFF ON THE RIGHT
SIDE
CAPT—AH THE WHOLE RIGHT SIDE IS GONE
ENG—FROM ABOUT ONE RIGHT BACK TO
AH
FO—ANYBODY

ENG—SOME PEOPLE ARE PROBABLY GONE—I
DON'T KNOW
CAPT—WE GOT A REAL PROBLEM HERE
FO—WE DON'T KNOW WHAT THE ####'S
GONNA HAPPEN WHEN WE START TO . . .
TOWER—UNITED EIGHT ELEVEN HEAVY
SEARCH AND RESCUE HAS LAUNCHED A HE-
LICOPTER INTERCEPT
FO—AH SAY AGAIN
CAPT—THEY LAUNCHED A HELICOPTER
TOWER—SEARCH AND RESCUE HAS
LAUNCHED A HELICOPTER TO INTERCEPT
AND AID YOU IN AH RETURNING BACK TO
HONOLULU

I wondered what Second Officer Thomas was thinking in the few minutes he spent surveying the damage
and I thought of Uncle Bud and his musings with me
many decades ago.

Uncle Bud often told me to trust the pilots because
they wanted to get down safely as much as I did. That
thought and Uncle Bud's face were crashing into the
forefront of my brain, along with the feeling that Uncle Bud was there with me, reminding me this highly
trained and capable crew were working hard to get us
all back safely.

Oh, and I prayed. Not the "Dear God, please bring
me a pony" kind of prayer.

Squeezing my eyes as tightly as I could, certain that

would help me focus and block out the bitter cold and the noise: "Dear God and any Angelic Beings: If anybody out there can hear me—please, please, please help the crew and help us return safely." Then I prayed it again. And again. And again. And again …

TOWER—UNITED EIGHT ELEVEN RUNWAY
FOUR RIGHT YOU'RE CLEARED TO LAND
CAPT—IS THAT THE LONGEST RUNWAY
FO—OKAY WE NEED A LONG RUNWAY
CAPT—I NEED A LONG FINAL
CAPT—TELL HIM WE NEED A LONG FINAL
FO—AND UNITED EIGHT ELEVEN HEAVY AH
WE'D LIKE AS LONG A FINAL AS YOU CAN
GIVE US
TOWER—UNITED EIGHT ELEVEN TURN AH
FIFTEEN DEGREES LEFT
FO—FIFTEEN LEFT NOW UNITED EIGHT
ELEVEN HEAVY
FO—OKAY I GOT LIGHTS OVER HERE
CAPT—OKAY
FO—OKAY YOU CAN SEE IN A MINUTE

Imagine my surprise during my prayers when in my mind's eye there appeared an enormous hand that swooped out of the clouds, under the aircraft, and gently brought support. At that moment, I felt and knew this Hand of God would bring us safely to a successful landing.

The scene was so realistic and out of character for me to see something that profound at a time like that, it startled me. My eyes flew open, as I fully expected to look out the hole and see we were supported by a large hand.

Suddenly, I was able to breathe. Relief, a great peace, awe, and confidence washed over me—a feeling of *I don't know how, and I don't know why, but I may soon witness a miracle.*

However, in reality, we were still losing altitude and drifting downwards toward the water.

I looked out the hole, straining to see in the distance, and there they were—the faint pinpoints of lights of Honolulu!

The cargo door malfunction occurred shortly after takeoff, approximately 100 miles outside of Honolulu. Seeing the island's lights, I felt relief that the flight crew had been able to turn this damaged aircraft around, and we were limping back. We had Honolulu in sight!

Perhaps this could be a rescue operation versus a retrieval. I prayed again, and that time, I also gave thanks for the distant lights and the slim possibility of survival.

We were getting closer and closer to the city lights, and even flying on two engines, we were losing elevation. However, we remained at an acceptable altitude.

TOWER—UNITED EIGHT ELEVEN I NEED AH SOULS ON BOARD IF YOU HAVE IT
FO—OKAY SOULS ON BOARD
FO—HOW DO THE CONTROLS FEEL
CAPT—ALRIGHT SO FAR

CAPT—OKAY WELL LET'S TRY THE GEAR
FO—OKAY TRYIN' THE GEAR
FO—YOU READY?
ENG—OKAY
FO—YOU'RE HIGH ON THE GLIDE SLOPE
CAPT—YEAH
FO—THAT'S FINE
CAPT—YEAH I WANNA BE HIGH
FO—TWO ENGINE APPROACH
ENG—I HEAR PEOPLE SCREAMIN' BACK THERE
CAPT—I THINK. . .
FO—SHE'S YELLING FOR 'EM TO SIT DOWN

When coming in for landing, the flight crew monitors air speed and altitude. However, in this situation, any altitude they lost could not be regained on two engines. A fully loaded 747 flying on two engines? You are going down.

With all the challenges and circumstances this crew faced, they decided to come in high and hot. The tower directed Captain Cronin to the longest runway which was 3,000 feet longer than the 12,000-foot-long Reef Runway. He would need every foot, as he was coming in faster than normal due to the lack of flap and rudder control. He was also factoring in the structural weakness of the damaged aircraft and that it could buckle when landing.

CAPT—WE GOT BRAKES?

ENG—NORMAL HYDRAULICS
FO—SO WE GOT BRAKES
FO—BUT YOU'RE ONLY GONNA HAVE RE-
VERSING ON ONE AND TWO

Meanwhile, in the dark and windy cabin, the flight attendants had only minutes to prepare themselves, the cabin, and the passengers for an inevitable ocean ditching and emergency evacuation. The flight crew fought to attach their face masks to their crew emergency oxygen bottles, then worked to help each other don life preservers. The crew also struggled with reduced visibility, the limited number of available megaphones, and overhead storage compartment doors breaking open. Several flight attendants attempted to demonstrate life jacket procedures. Others helped numerous passengers don their life preservers, including one flight attendant who helped about thirty-six passengers with their life preservers.

Other crew members worked to clear debris from the aisles and exit doors, then briefed "helper" passengers to assist in an evacuation. One flight attendant, standing at the front in the other aisle, was also screaming instructions into a megaphone.

Crew members held up passenger safety cards for passengers to review evacuation and life vest procedures, then used hand signals to convey the seated crash position—grab your ankles and keep your head down until the plane stops.

My entire seventeen-minute experience seated next to

the damage, the large hole, and the view ensured these final minutes would be unforgettable. Plus, coming in fast with only two engine reversers meant it would take a long time for the aircraft to stop.

Captain Cronin initiated a hard right turn that would pass muster with any fighter pilot. A turn so dramatic, if not strapped in, I'd have fallen out the hole. The angle nearly had me hanging in my seat, looking past the debris below me where the floor collapsed, directly into the ocean.

Seeing that, I realized these moments could be the last things I would ever see. Ignoring the crew's crash position instruction, I pulled myself into a sitting position and watched as we lined up with the runway.

While astounded we had made it to the point of an attempted landing, yet not fully convinced this aircraft had any chance of landing safely, it came to me that if these were my final moments, no way were they going to be spent with me tucked up against the seatback, staring at my own butt!

The aircraft lined up as we continued to fall out of the sky. Still flying over water, we approached the runway, about to fly over land, preparing to touch down. *Is this really happening? Are we really going to survive this?*

What chance did we have that this heavily damaged aircraft would hold together when it touched down? Structurally, would it hold up or snap apart where the fuselage was damaged and weakened?

What other damage was there? Landing gear, braking, stopping mechanisms? Would the braking system operate and engage? A fully loaded 747 normal landing speed is approximately 180 mph. It seemed we were coming in faster than a normal landing—but then I had never had an open window on a jumbo jet to get a sense of how fast a landing feels, so I chalked it up to that.

On final approach for the landing, fast and high, the crew had one shot at the runway. The crew was aware of the structural damage but didn't know what additional, hidden damage there might also be.

If the aircraft came in too low and missed the runway, the two working engines would be unable to generate enough thrust for this heavy aircraft to regain altitude for a second attempt. We would likely crash, as we would fly right into the edge of the runway.

If they came in too high and landed in the middle of the runway, would they be able to slow down, brake, and control the landing? Or would we crash at the end of the runway being unable to stop? This landing had to be precise.

But first? We must touch down and pray the aircraft would not break apart from the structural damage.

We were not out of the woods yet.

FO—LOOKS GOOD SO FAR

FO—ONE HUNDRED

FO—BRAKE PRESSURE'S AH HOLDING BRAKE

CAPT—LET'S GO THROUGH THE PROCEDURE
FO—BRAKE PRESSURE
CAPT—AS SOON AS I LOCK THE AH
ENG—SPOILERS ARE COMIN' IN
FO—OKAY
CAPT—I'M GONNA LOCK THE BRAKES
FO—OKAY HOLD ON
FO—AH SPEEDBRAKE PARKING BRAKE
ENG—SHUTDOWN THE ENGINES
FO—START LEVERS
CAPT—SHUT 'EM DOWN
CAPT—SPEED BRAKES
CAPT—WE'RE EVACUATING

We landed—and it was, even today, my best landing ever. Captain Cronin, a man of great faith, swears this was his best landing, certain this aircraft was truly in God's hands. He never wavered in his declaration that God landed that airplane.

After touching down and braking hard to a stop, the astounded passengers simultaneously burst into loud, raucous applause.

Stunned, I looked around at the passengers applauding, laughing, crying, and hugging each other. This celebration included many tears of joy as we rolled to a complete stop.

In all these years, even as I write this and "feel it," I have not been able to find words that describe the amazement, relief, and joy felt at not only what had happened—but that we survived.

Chapter Eleven

EMERGENCY LANDING
HONOLULU INTERNATIONAL AIRPORT

THE EMERGENCY EQUIPMENT and rescue vehicles raced alongside the crippled jet as the aircraft rolled to a full stop. The flight crew jumped into action, blowing the emergency doors and giving sharp commands at the slide evacuation point instructing passengers to leave behind all personal items, jump, and hit the ground and run away from the aircraft.

The orderly evacuation of the 328 remaining passengers down the slides was completed in forty-five seconds.

Every flight attendant suffered some sort of injury, from scratches to a dislocated shoulder, during either the flight or the evacuation.

My brain processed their last instruction to "hit the ground and run away from the aircraft"—so I did! I, along with 327 other highly motivated passengers, hit the ground and scattered.

To this former track and field athlete, it felt as though I ran halfway to the neighboring island of Kauai. Sprinting down the runway, I passed a small group of Hawaiian firefighters, fully suited for a catastrophic event. The rescue crew stood at ready near their fire engines and rescue equipment. As I ran past, I heard, "Hey, where you going?"

That statement uttered in a calm tone of voice, with the unmistakable local Hawaiian lilt, slowed and then stopped me in my tracks. Turning to look back at the speaker, I pointed at the chaos behind me, "Are you nuts? Do you not see where I am running from?"

That first responder's familiar strong Hawaiian voice of reason cut through the fog in my brain, which was responding only to the "run" instructions. That voice brought me back from the fight-or-flight instinct and survival mode where I had been during this entire surreal experience.

Suddenly a "click," and it all hit me—it felt like an eternity since I had departed this airport yet is had been only about thirty minutes since we took off. The emergency lasted about seventeen minutes, and then I was back—not dead, not drowning, not fighting sharks. I was alive.

Stopping to gulp in fresh air, I walked a few steps to stand alone, away from everybody. Another deep breath, and I willed myself to turn and face that aircraft positioned maybe 100 yards away on the tarmac. As I turned, I lifted my head and looked back on what still felt like a dream, and my eyes fixated on the massive hole in the fuselage. When I saw the enormity of the damage for the first time from the outside of the aircraft, I gasped. My legs, my brain, my entire being crumbled into a cross-legged heap on the tarmac.

It was early morning, and a soft, warm Hawaiian rain was falling. All flights were suspended during our landing attempt, rendering the airport eerily silent. In the background, the distant, slowly rising clamor of rescue teams and other sounds still felt strangely muted after being seated near the incoming hurricane force winds and only feet away from two screeching, burning 747 engines.

In the cool night air, the lights of the rescuers were far removed from my brain, as the sensations from the warm, gently falling rain felt like head-to-toe loving, soft angel kisses.

Sighing, I again deeply inhaled the fresh air while the sensation of a soft cocoon of downy angel wings enfolded and held me. Then these words gently repeated, again in my right ear, "It's OK, you're OK. YOU ARE OK."

Still seated cross-legged, collapsed, and too stunned to move, shivering from shock and the extreme cold wind that had been blowing on me, my head dropped to my chest, and I felt I could finally breath normally.

My senses slowly reconnected, my head was pounding, my eyes burning, my body aching, my brain short-circuited, much like the wires that were sparking in the damaged cabin, as all the emotions crashed over me, fast and hard. All these sudden sensations created a large lump in my throat, and I simply could not move.

The emotions jumbled from stunned, exhausted, vulnerable, scared, and confused to also exhilarated and so very grateful to be alive. Willing myself to lift my throbbing head to look back at the 747 with the hole in the right side, it felt as though time stopped.

Still sensing an angelic presence with me in the soft rain and hearing those words, I felt something shift in me. It was in that moment that I heard in my head, my own voice saying, *He's wrong.* I sat up a little straighter.

Then I heard, *I did OK.* I sat up a little more.

Taking a deep breath, my head came completely upright, *I am not an idiot.*

Each of these proclamations created a mental revelation which inspired me in that moment to be straighter and stronger. Another click in the shift and the proverbial light bulb came on ...

Had I behaved on that damaged aircraft as the helpless idiot I had been programmed to believe I was? Well, clearly that was not what had happened.

Rather than staying meek, brainless, and quiet, I

stepped up and did my best to help and support those around me.

Doing so, I instinctively reclaimed who I really was, the authentic me—not who I was told to be.

Right then, I felt the visceral flipping of a switch in me. I knew that those seventeen minutes from explosion to landing would from here on out have a magnificent and significant bearing on my life.

It dawned on me that in that definitive moment, I had been touched by something I could not explain. Even though I often did not know what would happen in the next thirty seconds, I knew I was alive and had somehow just embarked on a new and different journey.

Sitting tall and alone on that tarmac in the gentle Hawaiian rain, I bowed my head to truly and sincerely thank God for whatever it was that had just happened.

Following that moment, as I lifted my head, it felt as though the world slowly restarted. The entire scene shifted from the surreal back to real time.

After taking several deep breaths, I found the strength to gather myself and try to stand. Seeming to come out of the mist, several firefighters appeared and hurried over to assist me to my feet. One took my arm to steady me and several others walked with us, quietly talking with me as we moved slowly down the rain-spattered tarmac to the parked aircraft. Medical teams stepped in, as well as one of the flight crew members who noticed my uncontrollable shaking.

The flight crew member hurriedly walked over, placing an arm around my shoulder to step directly in front of me to see me face-to-face. She looked me square in the eye to watch how I answered her questions about how I was doing, what I needed.

My brain remained locked in the *what-the-hell-just-happened* fog, my only focus was on those missing people. Once I found my voice, all I could repeat to her was, "There were people in those seats, and now they're gone; we have to find them. How fast can we get a team out there to rescue those people?"

While repeating my concerns, she gently turned to guide me toward the medics. They, too, could not miss my shaking and shocked facial expression. They immediately provided a silver thermal blanket, which the crew member arranged snugly around my shoulders. Then gently, she pulled me close, holding me and securing the thermal blanket, "Oh, honey—you're in shock."

While my focus was on repeating the missing person report, her "you're in shock" comment stopped me cold. As an athlete and farm girl, I played hard and played hurt, so this "shock thing" as a diagnosis was something new to me. My automatic response, "I've never had shock; what do you take for shock?"

Here we go—my standard solution because there must be a pill or medication to make me feel better, whatever this "shock" thing might be.

THE STAFF AND FIRST responders began loading passengers on the Wiki-Wiki buses the airport used to shuttle passengers to the terminal. Passengers were off-loaded and directed to restrooms and pay phones in the terminal. Many began queueing up at the pay phone banks, coin in hand. One of the staff escorted me to the front of the line, so I was one of the first to call home.

With hands shaking, I used my left hand to guide my right hand, to drop the quarter into the pay phone slot. Then I dialed home.

With the time change at two thirty a.m. in Hawaii, it was six thirty a.m. in Denver. My unexpected call caught Mark at home, where his first words to me were not entirely unexpected.

With a stern and surprised, "What do you want?" he made it crystal clear: my call was both a disruption and a bother to his morning routine.

"Well, I'm calling from the Honolulu Airport. The 747 I was on just blew up all around me. I'm fine. You know what? I'm going to hang up now so somebody else here in line can call somebody they know who gives a shit."

And with that, I hung up on him—clearly, a shift had occurred in me.

Until that moment, in those exact circumstances, the former me would have apologized profusely for having disrupted him and his morning, then apologized again for being involved in the accident. "I'm sorry" were the two words I used most often around him. Until that moment, I had never spoken up, pushed back, or hung up on him in my life.

Little did I realize that since this entire event had just occurred, the news outlets weren't aware of or reporting on it. He was confused by what he had just heard, so he promptly called a local radio news station to ask about a United 747 plane crash in Hawaii.

Of course, the radio station knew nothing about it, and recognizing a scoop, the news team immediately chased the story and were breaking it during the morning rush hour drive time. He then contacted the rest of my family in Denver, and at first, they thought he was joking.

How could it be since I just left town, plus there was nothing on the news! He explained what he knew, and they realized this was no joke. Taking the day off work, they gathered and stayed together at our home as the story unfolded.

Mother-Vic and Dad were on a road trip exploring the western states. Traveling down the road, they tuned into the local radio station's morning news, where they learned a United flight from Honolulu to Auckland had experienced a major malfunction. While they considered it quite the coincidence there was a problem with a United flight running a similar itinerary, it never crossed their minds it was my flight, as their daughter was flying from Denver to Sydney.

Remember, there were no cell phones or personal

computers in 1989, so they knew nothing else and continued their trip until a routine check-in call with the family. When they learned the truth, they immediately returned to Denver.

After the rescue team and first responders directed passengers to the phone banks, those United 811 passengers seated away from the explosion were escorted to an open area along the terminal hallways. There, the rescue operation teams set up light provisions, blankets, pillows, and several cots. By then, normal airport operations and flights had resumed in and out of the busy Honolulu airport.

Other passengers walking past that quickly assembled passenger staging area saw stunned United 811 passengers lined up or leaning against the walls, quietly talking amongst themselves. A single, drooping line of yellow police tape was the only thing separating the United 811 passengers from the other passengers going about their business. Behind the thin line of sagging yellow tape, the meager accommodations, and blank stares on the faces of the survivors was undoubtedly a stark and somewhat disturbing sight to other passengers going about their business.

Those of us seated closest to the damage were separated and escorted to the United Red Carpet Room, where we were immediately handed off to a team of FBI agents.

Following the interviews with medical and other personnel, the passengers' options were to remain in Hawaii until they could travel, or they could return to their flight origination point, or they could continue on to their destination. United secured several hotel locations around the island so the stranded passengers' responses determined where they would be accommodated.

Given that my itinerary was a business trip to meet hundreds of clients in Sydney in a few days, with little thought, my decision was to take the next flight in order to continue on to my destination. Plus, being only slightly injured with cuts, scrapes, and bruises, I was determined to "get back on that horse."

When evacuating a damaged aircraft, passengers are instructed to not take anything or any personal belongings with them. Against those crew instructions, I grabbed my briefcase, and that's a big "no-no." My purse carrying valuable and sentimental jewelry, my ID and passport, and money had blown out during the decompression and was 100 miles away, floating somewhere in the Pacific Ocean.

During the airport interviews shortly after the incident, one of the United reps asked the value of those lost contents. At that moment, brain numbed and tired, my off-the-cuff estimate vastly undervalued the jewelry, plus I miscalculated the amount of cash I had carried. The rep advised me they did not know the status of my checked bags, whether they were still in the cargo hold of the aircraft, holding up the floor of the cabin, or if they had they been sucked out. They would advise me as soon as they knew, and if found, when those bags could be released.

In the meantime, United paid my transportation and hotel expenses in Hawaii, plus reimbursed me $200 in cash to cover my lost items. How I traveled internationally, both directions with no ID, I do not recall. It was a different time, so somehow arrangements were made that I could do so.

Chapter Twelve

**WAIKIKI AND SYDNEY, AUSTRALIA
THE WEEK OF FEBRUARY 24, 1989**

ENTERING MY SECOND FLOOR WAIKIKI hotel room that morning, I leaned on the back of the hotel door as I closed it. Relief flooded over me as I finally took a minute to just breathe. This was the first time I had a moment completely to myself in the last eight hours. Throwing open the balcony doors to take in the ocean view and inhaling the unique essence of the tropics, I smiled softly as I reconnected with the familiar scents and sounds of a Waikiki morning.

Sighing, I stepped onto the balcony and into the captivating harmonies of cars, buses, taxis, bicycles, and motor scooters as they rushed by on their way to work and touring adventures. Tourists' chatter also carried on the morning breeze, and across the street were the rhythmic sounds of the Waikiki Beach surf. Turning to reenter the room, I plopped down onto the side of the bed, and I could not move. My tired and aching body simply sat there, while I stared out at the beach with the bright Hawaiian sun, blue skies, the sounds of the surf, and all the normal morning activity all around me. My body was still, yet my mind reeled as it chewed on, *What the hell just happened here?*

Surveying the room, my eyes stopped on the telephone on the bed stand. Gritting my teeth, I stared down the phone, then reluctantly picked up the receiver to call my house.

At that point, nobody at home had a clue where I was or what was going on. Certain my immediate family was fully aware of the situation through news reports, they must be concerned and wondering how I was doing. While gathering my thoughts, I rationalized perhaps I had just been "a little stressed" when I called Mark the first time right after the incident and convinced myself that had to be why I had so rudely hung up on him.

In the calm and relative privacy of the hotel room, I was feeling more able to handle making another call. News sources continually interrupted regularly scheduled programs with breaking reports, photos, and interviews, so he could see what had happened.

Either way, Mark's reception on this second call was of more interest and far more concern. As was his nature, he had taken charge back home, telling me he had contacted and gathered family and friends. He then asked what else he could do to help me.

After his expressions of niceties and concern with my updates on my condition and location, I mentioned the $200 reimbursement from United for my lost purse and items. Just like that, Mark's switch flipped to full fury and a changed focus, "Two hundred dollars! That is ALL you fucking claimed and received for the jewelry and items. Goddamn it, Shari, THINK. Do you not have any fucking clue how expensive the jewelry is that I give you?"

That sealed it; no way was I rushing straight home to that.

My next call was to check in at the office. Mark had immediately updated the good people there, so when I checked in, friends clamored to speak with me before I was transferred to Randy, the travel agency owner, my immediate boss and friend.

Randy and his family offered to assist me in any way they could, first by strongly suggesting sending another representative to Sydney so I could return home. Or they would support me if I chose to continue on. After Randy and I talked, I explained to him that I was just fine, everything was good, and my choice was to carry on to my work in Australia.

Hanging up after all that talking and digging deeply to convince my loved ones that I was fine, my head began spinning. Once I hung up as the confident "I'm fine, really" to my family and friends, I felt a shift back to the real stress I was feeling.

Having convinced those closest to me that I was mostly certain about some things and very uncertain about other things, the truth was I was unsure and not fully trusting how I felt about anything. Like a load of bricks, it hit me that all I'd endured to this point really was too much.

Falling back onto the bed, lost in my thoughts, I stared up at the ceiling and recognized I needed to talk face-to-face with a friend. My first local call was to Sean, a former Denver coworker who lived and worked in Hawaii.

Sean answered his phone while he was eating breakfast; his wife was already out the door for work. We had about five seconds of, "Hello, great to hear from you, etc.," and then, "Heyyyyy, wait a minute. You weren't on that United flight that just blew up—the one out of Hawaii, were you?"

"Um, yeah. I was." Admitting, owning, and making it real choked me up, and I was unable to finish speaking.

Sean took over, "Where are you right this minute?" Then he asked what I needed. Sputtering and mumbling, I shared my hotel location and that I did not know what I needed. He asked me to stand by, that he would get back after calling his office to take the day off. He immediately called back with his plan to pick me up, get some food, and then, see whatever else I needed.

That man's kindness, concern, compassion, and sincere efforts to help me saved my life that day.

Having made that call, I had a plan and a friend. It was time to take a shower.

Since I can remember, shower water cascading over my head has been so healing for me. I cannot think in the mornings or get my groove on without having water cleansing my head. My "must-haves" are hot morning shower water over my head, a sunroof in my car, and either high or "funky" ceilings in my homes. I simply cannot function when the top of my head feels blocked. Weird, huh?

Undressing in the bathroom, I looked in the mirror at the reflection looking back, and it was not me.

There stood a very disheveled, pale, stressed looking woman with one large blue earring. Slowly focusing in on the one earring, I realized that when the debris blew past me, battering my head and shoulders, it took the other earring out the hole too.

That steamy, hot shower gently massaged my head, neck, and back, translating into pure bliss for my sore, aching body. I slowly felt myself going from simply numb to somewhat human as the warm water and the aroma of fresh-smelling soap loosened me up.

I was surprised to notice bruises starting to form across my hips, which seemed an odd place for bruising.

Then slowly, I realized that was where my seat belt had been. When the explosive decompression yanked me toward the hole, it pulled me against that unrelenting seat belt, holding me in the seat and saving my life.

While shampooing, I also discovered foreign objects in my hair. I began removing small pieces of cabin debris and shrapnel from my scalp, surprised there were more than a few cuts in my head, plus cuts and bruises on my shoulders that needed some attention to stop the bleeding.

After the shower, I realized I had no makeup or toiletry items other than the shampoo, soap, and toothbrush provided by the hotel. My luggage was still unaccounted for, and my personal carry-on items had been deposited into the Pacific Ocean, which meant I had nothing to wear except what I had been wearing since leaving Denver.

Wrapping one of the hotel's large, soft, fluffy towels around me, I gathered my only clothes and stepped back into the morning sun pouring over the balcony, thinking, *Thank you, Uncle Bud for Plan Bs.*

After laying my clothes on one of the balcony deck chairs to air out, my body collapsed into the other deck chair. With every breath of sea salt scented air, with the warm sun caressing my face and the gentle ocean breezes drying my hair, this was the first moment I felt good and safe.

Leaning back and stretching out in the chair, the towel slowly fell away, exposing my battered body to the healing warmth of the Hawaiian sun. Surf and sun are truly therapeutic for me. In my mind, and in that moment, I felt I had hit the jackpot and just maybe I could survive this.

My second floor, oceanfront balcony overlooked the increasing tourist foot traffic, and even through the fog of my brain, I chuckled softly at the bit of a commotion starting below. Normally, being naked on a second-floor balcony in Waikiki would be a significant consideration for me. However, that day, my give-a-shit meter registered at, "I do not care. I should be dead. Instead, I just took a hot shower, and now I'm healing by the ocean in the Hawaiian sun. If you want to arrest me? Go ahead. So what? I. Do. Not. Care."

In the short time it took for my hair to dry and my body to warm up, my clothes were somewhat air freshened. Sean called for me from the hotel lobby, and we sat there for a few minutes, discussing my choice to continue with the trip, which was rescheduled to depart later that evening. Sean insisted on driving me back to the airport later for the flight. He flat refused to just put me in a cab and send me back by myself.

That settled, next up was to repair my broken acrylic fingernail. Instinctively, I knew my need was to tackle and complete small tasks. It was surprising to me to recognize that simply showering and getting dressed, then meeting Sean, were at that moment significant accomplishments because until then, I had felt so lost, broken, and scattered.

Moving at far less than my usual 110-mph multitask speed, I realized my next small task was that nail repair. It was important for me to make the repair to feel the pieces "of me" were being put back together. Instinctively, and at some level of my psyche, managing those small tasks gave me a glimpse that someday maybe I would be whole or "normal" again. Interesting what your thinking, focus, and priorities become during times of significant trauma.

Sean then declared it was his turn to select the next task and whisked us a few blocks away to the beautiful, historic Halekulani Hotel and restaurant, located on the beach at Waikiki.

Waikiki Beach is recognized by the Hawaiians to be a place of hospitality and healing, and the beach is known to them for its healing waters. The original Halekulani was built in 1883, and the locals named the location Halekulani or "House befitting Heaven".

There was healing going on in several levels for me as he secured a table by the hotel pool, facing the beach. The pool is famous for the beautiful orchid mosaic on the pool bottom, which was handmade with 1.2 million pieces of glass tile, so the setting he chose was sheer perfection.

We ordered several strong gin and tonics while we enjoyed *saimin*, a local noodle soup favorite. It was so very relaxing as we sipped on the cool drinks and enjoyed good food in the beautiful Hawaiian surfside location. This was perfect—talking with my friend, enjoying unfettered time under an umbrella next to the healing waters of Hawaii.

With the food, refreshments, and all the activity of the past twenty-four hours, a deep exhaustion simply washed over me, and to say I was feeling very tired was putting it lightly. My next request was to return to the hotel to rest before the flight that night. Sean arranged the time to pick me up to escort me back to the airport.

After walking me to the hotel lobby Sean pointed me towards the elevators. I tiredly shuffled to my room. Standing at the door, unlocking it, I was barely able to push the door open and collapsed on the bed. Then, big surprise, I was unable to sleep!

As mentally and physically exhausted as I was, my eyes simply would not close. Laying there, I took a deep breath and exhaled, gently closing my eyes—they popped right back open. *What?*

Taking another deep breath, I again gently closed my eyes, and again they popped open. I soon tired of fighting it; as exhausted as I felt, I certainly did not understand why I could not close my eyes. All that remained was to surrender and simply lay there listening to the sounds of Waikiki until five p.m., and then it was time to head back to the airport.

Sean was clearly a little anxious, and I was unsure what I was feeling, other than sarcastically grateful for the mind and body numbing lack of sleep, as that took the edge off my stress. Or did it?

Arriving a little early, I easily checked in for the flight. Realizing we had time to walk over to an airport tiki bar, we claimed two of the eight empty seats at the small bar with a TV on the small back wall. There were so many jumbled thoughts and emotions going through my head as I was trying not to think about the upcoming second-shot-at-making-it-to-Sydney flight. Then, upon landing, thinking about getting back to work after losing a day with this darn "inconvenience."

Lost in thoughts of pending work tasks, my brain strained to think in my usual express mode while the rest of me was just barely keeping up. The other side of my brain was reminding me to just stop and enjoy this little respite time here in Hawaii before getting into the crazy work pace.

Sipping our drinks, Sean and I nervously chatted until they interrupted a TV program with a news bulletin—"Update . . . United 811 . . . *nine people perished . . . so far, two of the missing people have been located . . . identified two types of body tissue in the right side engines . . .*"

Gasping, my brain disconnected from the remainder of the report; my thoughts were replaced with a loud buzz in my head. Words became gibberish, and an immediate tightness grabbed my chest. My throat was closing as my hands flew to my mouth. I couldn't breathe. Everything around me faded away, and I was left in another place, oblivious to my surroundings. Sean leaned forward, deeply concerned, yet unsure of what to do.

All my jumbled emotions tumbled out hearing that news. All the feelings for those people who perished, for the survivors who were terrified, for the heroic flight crew, for me ...

This was the first time I cried. My elbows on the bar, my head in my hands, as my head was shaking back and forth. Tears were running down my face, "No. Oh, no. No." That news again showed me I was not making any of this up; this crazy experience was all real. Now I knew the fate of at least two of the passengers, and I was gutted. Sobbing, I knew I needed that release to allow all the anguish, terror, and confusion to just flood out.

Sean consoled me as the young lady bartender came over, quietly asking if everything was all right.

Even in my fog, hearing her words motivated me to compose myself. Breathing deeply, I worked to manage the enormous lump in my throat and pull it together. Finally, I was able to explain I had been a passenger on that flight, and I was about to board a flight to continue on to Sydney later that night.

We three continued to quietly talk, and this lady graciously personified true Hawaiian-style hospitality. She calmed me by reaching across the bar to hold and pat my hands as she offered authentic compassion and concern to both Sean and me.

Words and thoughts were spilling out of me about why the news report rattled me so much. Nervously babbling, I tried to find the words to share the distress I felt because, for some reason, I had made the effort to really see and recognize those people when I boarded— and to know the fate of two of those people. Does that mean the seven other passengers endured a four-minute fall to the ocean and could have been alive as they were falling? That horrific thought further saddened and dismayed me.

Gasping, I stopped talking. It hit me that what I just spoke for the first time was another foggy memory surfacing for me—that when I was finally seated and settled, for some reason, it was really important for me to look at and acknowledge all the people around me. At that time, my reasoning was, I am going to be with these people for eight hours. Even if I don't speak with them, I can at least acknowledge their presence on this flight.

As much as I traveled, that thought had never before entered my head. My routine, like most everybody else, was to board, sit down, buckle up, and read your book. When I realized and said out loud that I made an extra effort to acknowledge and "see" them, that act alone was far different from my normal flight routine. Why did I do that? And then to learn the fate of two of them? Yes, I was rattled.

Watching the clock, Sean suggested it was time we walked to the gate. We said goodbye to the wonderful bartender, shared hugs, and she offered to comp our drinks, wishing us both much Aloha and best wishes.

Gathering my few remaining personal belongings, Sean and I walked in relative silence to the gate.

Again, I was one of the final passengers to check in. By then, feeling even more tired, stressed, and as though this was all happening in a dream, I floated through a totally surreal boarding procedure. Was I having an out-of-body experience?

Rather than the usual upbeat gate agent greeting, this United agent gently acknowledged me, consulted the seating chart, then solemnly handed me my boarding pass—seat 9F.

Seeing the boldly lettered 9F seat assignment, I was stunned—too stunned to protest, rather reverting to my keep-quiet-and-don't-say-anything mode.

Taking a big gulp, I turned to say my final goodbye and share my immense gratitude to Sean for all his hospitality and concern during my unexpected day with him. He gave me a big hug, then watched as I slowly moved toward the jetway door with the Auckland destination. I entered the quiet, desolate jetway tunnel toward another United 747.

Drifting solo down the jetway, my body and mind slipped into autopilot. With a strong sense of déjà vu, every sound, smell, and sensation piqued my senses during the surreal and dreamlike trek.

Pausing and taking a big, deep breath before stepping across the threshold into this 747, I entered and turned to my left into the then-familiar business class section.

In the few seconds it took to arrive at seat 9F, my hands were sweating, and my body began trembling as I stood there, looking at that seat. Fighting back tears, my head involuntarily shaking no, it was clear there was no way I could be in that seat.

I looked up, searching for the nearest flight crew member. I could see the many empty seats in this section. Apparently, the majority of the previous business class passengers elected to stay in Honolulu or return to their originating city. This section was nearly full on the original flight, and only five Business Class passengers chose to continue on. It was apparent all five of us were experiencing difficulty taking our same originally assigned seats.

One of the passengers motioned to a flight attendant, advising her there was "no way" any of us would be sitting in the same seats. Of course, the flight crew offered no objection to his request, so we five passengers gathered to sit together in the middle of the Business Class section.

This United flight crew was flown in from the mainland for our second attempt. The crew worked extra hard to take care of us from the minute we arrived at the gate, checked in, and boarded. Their extreme efforts at kindness and attentiveness to our needs, although well-intentioned, were becoming a bit much.

Prior to pushing back, another of the many flight attendants asked us for the fifteenth time how she could help us. Quietly but firmly, I offered that perhaps she did not realize it, but while we welcomed their attention and concern, their hovering was making us uncomfortable. Though their extra efforts were appreciated, I asked her to please stop and make this flight as normal as possible.

My unwillingness to speak up on my seat assignment and then to turn around and offer a strong suggestion regarding their cabin service, rather than being told what to do and complying, was another significant shift for me. That I felt confident enough to take a stand and do something about it was new territory for me.

She was somewhat startled, then apologetic. Always professional, she appreciated my directness, and I appreciated that we all found a way to do this because not only were we, the passengers, on edge. Clearly, the replacement cabin crew was as well.

The crew secured the cabin and closed the doors to push back as our small group looked at each other, grateful that we all understood the significance of the next 30 minutes. Falling silent as the aircraft was being secured for takeoff, I closed my eyes, wondering what could possibly happen next.

Everything about this flight was routine and normal as we pushed back and launched.

Our small group, and I'm certain other passengers as well, remained laser focused on the flight indicator screen at the front of the cabin that monitored the speed, altitude, and direction, as well as showing flight progress on the map, etc.

Climbing out, we all breathlessly watched the monitor, fixated on it as we reached 20,000 feet. Still climbing, my heart raced harder, and our nervous chatter became louder as we moved up to 21,000 feet. Reaching 24,000 feet, we all sat in silence, watching, internally reflecting on the situation we had experienced at this juncture mere hours earlier. This small group of surviving passengers remained hushed and introspective as we finally reached cruising altitude.

Feeling relieved to have made it to this point, we quietly resumed talking amongst ourselves about our own experiences and what awaited us when we landed. It was apparent that none of us could sleep, so for the next eight hours, we shared stories about selves, families, work, and other small talk to distract us from our own thoughts. After a short layover in Auckland to eat something and stretch our legs, several of us then continued on to Sydney.

A small group of senior United representatives traveled with us on this flight to assist the passengers to their destinations. When we landed in Sydney, those representatives helped me check into my Sydney hotel and made suggestions for local shops where I could purchase necessary personal items and fresh clothes.

Having endured the stress of that long trip, and finally alone in my Sydney hotel room, bone-tired, I perched on the side of the bed. Rather than stuffing my feelings and carrying on, I allowed myself to sit in the overwhelmingness of it all, dazed at the realization that I was finally and really in Australia.

Grasping that, along with the significant time change and trying to wrap my head around the impact of the International Date Line, not only was I exhausted, calculating the current day and time was confusing. So, what day was it?

Looking around the quiet, sunny room, my gaze drifted over to my meager belongings scattered on the bed. Sighing, I realized it would be good to get some fresh air, so my best course of action was to step out to the recommended shops to gather a few things before I started work early the following morning.

Walking out the hotel front door into the bustle and sounds of downtown Sydney instantly revived my tired, foggy mind and body. The liveliness of the people walking briskly was invigorating; cars, buses, and taxis flew by. Merging into the pedestrian flow, my pace picked up, and my focus became walking and watching the Aussie's pattern of navigating on the opposite side of the road.

I enjoyed the sunshine and the normal conversations in the lovely Australian accent spoken all around me.

I was also grateful for the locals who grabbed my arm, my shoulder, or the back of my collar to pull me onto the curb and out of traffic during my attempts to cross a street. After all, I was still looking in the "American" direction versus the "Aussie" direction when crossing, and it would have been ironic to have been hit by a bus because I looked the wrong way.

My first shopping discovery revealed Australia was expensive. The $200 barely allowed me to purchase one inexpensive skirt and top, plus a few personal items. My hope was that if my luggage still existed, it would arrive soon.

Clutching my few purchases, I wandered into a small, local shop to sample an authentic, delicious meat and gravy filled flaky Australian meat pie. Savoring that treat while seated at a window-front snack bar watching the city activity, it hit me that I was tired, my stomach was full, and my tasks were completed. I was ready to head back to hotel for a shower and rest.

Entering the sunlit room, the daylight slowly began fading into a late afternoon haze, and it would soon be dusk. Soothed by the warm shower and a full stomach, my even more tired and aching body was ready for much-needed rest. Drying off after the shower, I felt certain a sound sleep would rejuvenate me for the long workday tomorrow. However, it was not to be.

Burrowing down into the clean, fresh sheets and fluffy pillows, slowly taking deep breaths, I waited for sleep, but my eyes simply would not close. Darkness descended on the city, and for the first time, being in the dark was making me very uncomfortable.

My heart began racing harder, my head began throbbing and pounding, and I was more than uncomfortable, being in the dark absolutely unnerved me. Nearly frantic, struggling to breathe, I worked to halt my rising anxiety from engulfing me.

Finally, springing out of bed like a freed caged animal, I raced to the wall light switch. The moment the switch flipped turning the room from dark to light, my heavy breathing and anxiety came down a notch. This was all new for me; never had I "lost it" and certainly not because I was simply in a strange, dark hotel room.

Returning to the side of the bed, deeply breathing, I willed the anxiety to go away, thinking maybe I could sleep if the light was left on. After about five minutes of this self-talk, I again tried to burrow down and sleep. Nope—my eyes remained wide open.

Turning off the main light and leaving the smaller lamp across the room lit, I lay there, staring at the ceiling, frustrated, and exhausted. My first night in Australia was spent wide-awake in a lit room, immersed in thoughts about my journey to Sydney and what my first day at work might look like.

I knew it would be a busy day, starting when we met with the team to go over any last details and then begin the meet and greet of our incoming clients. The grounds team would transport buses of clients from the airport to the hotel where we would greet them, answer questions, check them in, and then get to work showing them Australia.

As long as there was no sleep for me, there was no need for a clamoring alarm clock to jar me awake. Since I was wide-awake, I arrived extra early the next morning to gather with our team at the hotel to welcome the incoming guests.

While the United 811 incident was blaring all over the news, our team was focused on assisting guests amid the usual energy and excitement of their arrival chatter.

A good number of these folks knew each other and were quite animated as they enjoyed a cold, local beverage, got reacquainted, and made plans.

In the hum of excited, exhausted travelers, there were also many fragments of conversation relating to United 811. One group came in on the same United flight that day and wondered how the survivors of yesterday's flight were doing.

I heard snippets about how happy they were to have not taken the same flight yesterday. "How horrible that must've been; how do you get on a plane after something that; don't know if I could ever fly again; I saw pictures on TV and how it landed safely, I'll never know," and so forth over and over again as each bus deposited new arrivals into the hotel lobby.

One conversation I overheard was a couple traveling with a fellow from Atlanta to Honolulu to Sydney. The man simply could not reboard in Honolulu onto Sydney. When they arrived at the departure gate, he was shaking and sweating before blurting out, "No way; I can't do this." With that, he turned and practically ran down the Honolulu concourse for the next flight back to Atlanta.

Numb, tired, and operating on auto-pilot, I remained focused on doing my best to handle the matters of our very wound-up clients. Our team was fully aware of my situation, yet there was no reason for them to mention it, nor for me to insert myself into the guests' United 811 conversations.

Because I'd been repeatedly told by Mark to "keep my fucking mouth shut," it wasn't difficult for me to keep quiet and stay out of the picture, saying nothing about my part in that event.

When any of the conversations were directed my way, it was best to simply nod, smile, and move to another spot. These insurance professionals worked very hard to earn trips, and my responsibility was to ensure all went smoothly for them. There was no reason to interject anything that could possibly alarm or frighten them for their long ride home.

However, during the entire week, my work was affected; I was distracted, tired, distraught, and working extra hard not to show it. Through gritted teeth, I continually reminded myself, "Keep quiet; nobody wants to hear what you have to say anyway."

With all the noise, endless excited chatter, laughter, and the constant reminder of United 811, I often needed to step away. When I felt myself slipping, my voice would begin changing; hot tears would well up in my eyes. Blinking hard, I would force a smile while my throat began to close. Feeling my head start to pound from my clenched teeth, I would begin sweating, and it was all I could do to turn and gracefully bolt from the commotion.

At that point, my solution was to slip away to my hotel room sanctuary to sit quietly in the chair I placed in front of my window looking out over Sydney.

My salvation was plopping down into that chair, taking a few minutes to sit and stare out the window at the normal world on the other side of the wall, telling myself I was safe in the room and would someday soon be able to return to that world "out there."

But at that moment, I needed a few minutes to catch my breath and focus. Simply functioning and acting normal was harder than I ever imagined, and it required most of my attention.

In the midst of the first day arrival scene, the local Sydney newspaper contacted me to arrange an interview. The reporter and I met in my room for the interview and photos. While reviewing the incident timeline for the reporter, it hit me I had not slept in something like sixty hours. Looking at the article's photo of the tired, rough-looking woman gazing out the window certainly confirmed that.

My gratitude that I survived to the end of that first workday was immeasurable. Finally, every guest was accounted for, all their luggage issues had been resolved, everybody was safely transported to and checked in the hotel, the welcome/mixer cocktail party and speeches were concluded, and the guests were on their own to party and get ready for a busy day two.

Shuffling to my room, it was all I could do to prepare for sleep. One thing about this job, we ensured all loose ends were tied up at day's end, meaning we were the last ones to bed. Because we were responsible for arranging the next day programs, starting with breakfast, we were also the first to rise. Those responsibilities were a formula for long days and very short nights.

Entering my room, I carefully removed my one new outfit, which constituted my entire work wardrobe. Giving it a quick check for spills or significant laundry challenges, and seeing none, I hung it up to refresh for tomorrow. Showering and pre-bed small chores accomplished, I fell into bed with the bedside lamp on.

My aching head nestled onto the soft pillow, and perhaps this night, I could finally and slowly relax.

Turning to shut off the bed stand light, my arm stopped halfway to the switch. It was surprising to me how unsettling the dark of night had become. I couldn't do it. I could not reach over to shut off the room light—or my brain.

My mind started whirring between the relative normalcy of today's work to the crazy emotions racing around in my head.

Am I dead? I must be dead because I am so lightheaded, and this does not feel like me. This is not real. Maybe I really did die on that flight, and I'm in some alternative universe. Or like in movies when the dead person doesn't realize they're dead. That has to be what is going on because there is no way we survived that. OK, OK, but if I am alive, what do I do with this new/different me?

One voice in my head was carrying on a conversation with the other voice in my head, and a third voice chimed in to remind me that hearing many voices in one's head is what crazy people do.

In my exhausted state, my anxiety quickly took off as my heart began to race even harder, and it became difficult to swallow, as my throat was closing on me.

Startled and frightened, I bolted straight up in bed because everything felt "off." I was vividly remembering the recent chaos and terror on United 811. An indescribable and visceral fear suddenly overtook me.

Am I nuts? Why should I ever again think everything is OK?

It happened once; it could happen again, even in this seemingly safe hotel room. Can something I could never, ever imagine happen again and once again change my life? Or maybe this time it will kill me?

Will I ever be able to trust that I can relax, feel comfortable, and feel safe again?

All these thoughts were crashing into each other in my brain, and I was unable to bring them to a stop or even form some kind of a conclusion. They kept coming at me faster and louder, and then I forced myself to accept the facts of my current situation.

I was in a strange country, hearing strange accents,

handling strange money, and eating strange food. I had no ID, purse, clothes, or even my toothbrush. I was in a strange hotel room in a strange bed, and I did not see or have anything familiar around me; I didn't know where I was or even who I was.

I hadn't slept in days. Plus, with the time change and crossing the International Date Line, I didn't even know what day it was, what time it was, and for a second, couldn't recall what city I was in.

Feeling I was about to get really frantic, I looked around the room for anything familiar to focus on and ground me. I told myself, whether I was dead or alive, *For Pete's sake get a grip; take a minute and breathe.*

One of the voices convinced me to take several deep breaths to clear my foggy brain, and then I began repeating a mantra out loud in different voice tones and inflections, "Shari, get your SHIT together. Shari, GET your shit together. SHARI, get your shit together. Shari, get your shit TOGETHER."

Sitting there in bed, shaking and sweating, heart pounding, I heard the sound of my own voice as it talked me off the ledge. I was somewhat convinced that if I really was dead, I wouldn't be able to speak out loud or hear my own voice, right? Again, I had to come up with *something* that made sense to me.

Feeling myself slightly calm down, I worked to assess the situation. What was clear to me was this anxiety, while slightly lowered, remained.

Taking stock of the situation, it was glaringly apparent sleep was going to be a challenge, and for sure, I would never sleep if the light was off.

In need of a new plan, "we" (all my voices) agreed to move the lamp to the other side of the room for a more indirect light, then give sleep another try. Moving the lamp, I returned to bed only to discover my eyes still would not close. However, as the very short remainder of the night wore on, it seemed I "rested deeply," though often startled enough to sit up and look around. After assuring myself I was safe, I would then lay back and deeply breath. This pattern continued until it was time to rise.

For the next few days, my routine became rising early, taking care of the day's work and challenges, returning to the room, and preparing my one work outfit for the next day and myself for bed.

The dark absolutely terrified me so the light stayed on. However, even a dimly lit hotel room is not conducive to good sleep. At night, as I ran through this routine, I worked in my head to understand or put words to my new deep, primal insecurity and anxiety.

Breaking it down, my only conclusion was that being in a dark room with lights off was simply not an option.

FOR YEARS, I WAS ASKED so many times if I should have done it differently and not immediately gone on to Australia? Should I have stayed in Hawaii a few days?

Or even just turned around and gone home?

One hundred percent of the time, even in retrospect, my deeply felt conviction is, "No—my nature is to soldier on and see this out."

Knowing my profound, primal connection to the ocean, had I remained even a few days longer near those healing waters of Hawaii, I would quite likely still be there.

Not that living in Hawaii again was a bad thing. Deep down, I knew I had to keep moving. Had I remained in Hawaii, I likely would not have faced and handled whatever this shift initiated in me.

One of my favorite quotes is from Alfred, Lord Tennyson: "The shell must break before the bird can fly."

Had I stayed in the nice, comfortable, familiar shell of Hawaii, clearly not only my life, but also my "self" and my circumstances would have evolved differently.

We all receive little cosmic nudges or random experiences that result in wake-up calls that move us in various directions. Or not.

Me? Seldom do I receive little wake-up calls. My nature is to be moving in many directions at once, meaning I often miss or ignore those nudges, maybe even step over them. That is, until I need the Big Kahuna kind of wake-up to get my attention. United 811 was The Big One, and it was time to take notice.

At that point, determining up from down, left from right, night-light on or light off, made me realize it was serious reset time for me. My psyche and soul were much like a newly hatched chick, and I instinctively knew my best option was to "go with it," in order to discover why all these synchronicities and United 811's miraculous landing offered me another chance at life.

Why me? This journey could have been an ending for me; rather, it was a new beginning.

A few short days prior, my focus had solely been on the hot-and-cold environment of my home life. Now, by surviving the recent experiences and beginning my recovery in a completely unfamiliar environment, I focused on my confusion about what to do with this "new me" that survived. This all became front and center in my thinking.

All things considered, getting back on the horse was not only my best option, but at that point in my life, my only option.

On the third day of the conference, things were going smoothly for the group, and I managed to create some semblance of a routine. Even with the night-light burning, there was some sleep coming to me, helping to clear the fog in my brain.

That third day ended with my anticipation of wonderful, quiet solitude in my then-familiar hotel room. As I walked the hallway to my room, I paused at the door, sighing and taking a deep breath. Unlocking the door, pushing it open with my shoulder to enter, my eyes immediately fixated on a significant difference in the room. Boldly placed in the middle of the floor were my two pieces of missing luggage.

My hands flew to my face, as this sight stopped me in my tracks. Gasping, my body began shaking, and my internal voice wondered if this was that "shock" thing happening again. Unable to move, I could not take my eyes off those two pieces of luggage that became the elephant in the room.

To this day, I don't know why seeing those two bags simply paralyzed me. Standing there, staring at them, the nagging question if they had gone out the hole in the explosion was answered, leaving only the musing and wonder of what part of holding up the collapsing aircraft floor had they played, if any.

Stunned, I glared at the welcome-unwelcome intruders that abruptly invaded the small semblance of normalcy I had worked so hard to create the past three days.

Standing there as seconds passed, I felt myself moving from the heart pounding, ragged breathing, shaking hands to willing myself to "get it together." Taking another deep breath, even I had no idea what was about to happen next.

Slowly and deliberately, I took a step toward the bags like an animal stalking its prey, watching them out of the corner of my eye as I gingerly walked around them to the other side of the room. Reaching the side of the bed, I collapsed and worked to compose myself and grasp what had just happened.

Even as I felt my throat closing, eyes watering, and

felt the room begin to spin, I could not stop staring at the luggage. Surrendering to all the emotion tied to seeing those bags, I lay back on the bed, then shifted to my side in order to maintain eye contact and watchful curiosity over those two bags.

Unsure how much time had passed, maybe several minutes, my head was clearing, and I pushed myself to a sitting position. Unsurprisingly, there was one thing I was very certain about. I was unable to touch or open those bags, reducing their existence in the middle of the room from my previously lost and mysterious luggage to simply another piece of hotel furniture to walk around.

During this Australian tour, the convention moved to several locations. The bellhops and ground transportation personnel handled all the luggage, and unless absolutely necessary, those bags remained virtually untouched by me. And yes, I washed and wore my one Sydney purchased outfit the entire trip, until I was finally able to convince myself to open the bags in order to select another outfit for this next chapter in my life, the return flight home.

Chapter Thirteen

AT THE CONCLUSION OF THE client convention, my focus turned to the journey home, which would originate from our final Australian destination, Cairns, back to Sydney. After this very hectic week, I was feeling apprehensive about the return flight. There would be no stopover in Hawaii on this flight. This would be my first ever fifteen-hour nonstop experience, and it would be fifteen long hours traveling from Sydney to Los Angeles, on yet another United 747.

For the Sydney–Los Angeles leg, I was assigned a seat located in the first row, on the right-side aisle in the middle seats of the coach section.

Settling in after boarding, it was clear my four seat-mates to my left and I would need to crane our necks upwards in order to view the large movie screen on the back of the bulkhead that was visible to the entire section. On the plus side, the seat placement facing the bulkhead did provide welcome extra leg room.

As we nestled in, the crew announced they would be serving three meals and showing four movies during this fifteen-hour nonstop flight.

I absentmindedly observed the passengers while the crew hustled to prepare the cabin, closing and locking the overhead bins and finally closing the cabin doors. The jumbo jet pushed back from the jetway and turned toward the runway. My mind was reeling from the events of the past week as the fully packed 747 lumbered into our launch position.

Closing my eyes, lost in these reflections, I attempted to clear my thoughts and absorb that it was just over one week ago everything was fairly "normal" in my life and I was simply heading out for a routine business trip.

Could it be that in just nine days, everything for me had changed? But what exactly had changed? Better yet, what would I do with these changes?

My thoughts began coming at me, faster and faster, in sync with the aircraft picking up speed to begin this roll-liftoff-no-turning-back-now long haul flight back to Los Angeles.

THE LARGE AIRCRAFT GENTLY rose higher as we departed Sydney. Looking across the aisle into the window, I watched as the Australian coastline disappeared from sight. We gained speed, achieving cruising altitude with all systems normal.

Still gripping my armrests, the young man seated to my left asked if everything was OK. Hearing the concern in his voice broke into my thoughts, and frankly, it startled me to hear a new voice in my head. I turned to face him, certain his first look at my exhausted demeanor and tired, sunken eyes would also concern him.

He mentioned he noticed I was gripping the seat and shaking. Was everything OK? Not wanting to unnerve him if he happened to be an already nervous flyer, all I briefly shared was that my original flight from Honolulu to Australia did not go well and that was perhaps why this fifteen-hour return flight had me a bit nervous.

He gently patted my left hand, which was maintaining a death grip on the armrest between us, and correctly guessed what was going on with me. Replying in his lovely Australian accent, "Ah, I read about that flight. Good on you for surviving, and what a great story." He went on to calmly assure me that he understood my anxiety, wished me a comfortable flight, and even though he was exhausted, to please not hesitate to wake him should I need anything. With that, he pulled the small airline blanket high up on his chest and quietly dozed off.

After approximately forty-five minutes into the flight, one side of my brain was still working to convince the other side of my brain to "get a grip." At least "they" recognized my only responsibility for the next fourteen hours and fifteen minutes was to simply sit there. After all, so far, there was nothing unusual in the flight.

My brain finally accepted the situation, allowing my body to release some of the tension and stiffness in my shoulders that felt tight all the way up to my ears!

While my senses remained on high alert, there was a subtle shift as the 747 engines made some sort of adjustment. They sounded different, and the aircraft felt as though it mushed back or slowed down a bit. The throttled back engine sound and slight shift in the aircraft instantly had me internally gasping, *Oh, crap. Here we go again . . .*

Walking past me on my right was one of the flight crew members checking passengers and filling requests. As calmly as possible for me in that moment, my reflexes caused me to reach out and stop her. In a voice I believed to be calm, however, I'm certain she detected a degree of panic, I said, "What's wrong? What just happened!"

With a puzzled look, she leaned in closer to ask if everything was OK. Hearing those words and the genuine concern in her voice, all I had been holding back came rushing out. Speaking quietly so as not to create a scene, I briefly described my stress, due to my recent experience on United 811.

"Ah," was all she said and invited me to join her in the galley. With pulse and heart racing, my brain quickly sized up her simple offer of help. My tired and stressed mind struggled briefly with the entire situation because, in order to join her in the galley, I would have to unbuckle my seat belt. *Can I even do that right now?*

Taking a deep breath, I reached down to unclick the belt and felt unnerved as the small sense of security the seat belt provided slipped away. I was moving on automatic pilot; that I could, and would, unbuckle my seat belt to stand up to move about the cabin both surprised and terrified me.

Taking another deep breath, while pushing down on the armrests to stand, I took the few steps required to reach and turn left to enter the galley behind the bulkhead. My every movement was deliberate and in slow motion as I stepped into the galley, away from the other passengers. Moving the six feet to finally reach my destination, I leaned back onto the high counter with my hands behind me, gripping the ledge. Standing there, we talked for some time. Flight crew members came by, and she somehow subtly indicated with a hand or head movement the sign to give us some privacy.

Patiently, she initiated small talk and then slowly began explaining at that point of the flight, the cockpit crew were simply adjusting the engines for the appropriate cruising speed. She maintained her composure, as though she showed every passenger this amount of personal time for flight operation explanations and a tour.

She then suggested showing me around the galley, where she explained how the hot food for more than 300 meals, for three different mealtimes, was prepared by crew members on the deck below. She explained the dumb waiter that brought the hot meals from the kitchen below up to the galley for serving and how the fifteen-hour flight required two complete flight crews to remain legal by splitting the flight time.

We walked over to the area where the off-duty crew rested during the flight. She opened the door of the crew rest lounge to view the double rows of bunks attached to the walls. She and I were chuckling like a couple of long-lost friends as she asked me to imagine the amount of trash generated by nearly 400 people on a fifteen-hour, nonstop flight. She then described how near the end of the flight, their trash area was packed, and the overflow was placed into this room. By the time they land, the floor of their sleeping area was often full of trash bags. We talked about her job and the wonderful destinations she visited, both for work and for fun.

As a professional flight crew member, she was trained to manage stressed travelers. The conversation and her friendliness made the time go by and was helpful in calming me. She focused on topics to distract me from my anxiety. She did not ask or talk about the United 811 incident. For that, I was grateful.

Never feeling rushed or that I was her "problem

passenger," after about 30 minutes, we reached a point I felt confident enough to return to my seat. Plus, she needed to return to her crew duties.

Following a movie or two, plus at least one meal, we were seven hours into the flight, a long time to be in one seat, and we were not even halfway to Los Angeles. Looking at my watch, I shook my head wondering, *How will I ever make it through eight more hours?*

As those last eight hours passed, I remained snuggly strapped in my aisle seat, tired and sorting through all the many different emotions, while all around me was a blur of meals, movies, and small talk with my seatmate when he woke to eat or stretch.

While there was no sleeping for me, my relief and excitement peaked when the flight crew announced we were nearing Los Angeles and minutes away from our final approach. Yay! I was giddy at the sight of endless ocean transitioning to land as we flew over the West Coast.

The five-thirty a.m. early morning arrival in Los Angeles allowed me approximately two hours connection time to walk around the terminal a bit to stretch my legs before I boarded the flight to Denver. Tired and emotionally exhausted, walking about the familiar Los Angeles Airport felt as though I was sleepwalking and dreaming.

At one point, I stopped to lean against a wall to just take it all in, certain I looked like a pale ghost as I watched people moving about normally. Taking in the sights and smells of early morning coffee, people speaking

American English, people rushing by, simply doing what they do in an airport, my sense of, *What just happened?* continued to roll around in my head. My feelings were even more conflicted and confused as I confirmed to myself how "different" I felt and how "different" I was. Even though I was not yet able to understand what and how, I just knew it.

We finally boarded for the short two hour and twenty-five minute familiar flight home, which gave me a strong pull of comfort, much like a cow to the barn at days' end. Following the fifteen-hour over water flight, I looked out in wonder while the flight crossed the vastness of the wide-open western states.

From my aisle seat, I looked past the other passengers to gaze out the windows at beautiful desert landscapes, then the Rocky Mountains. Finally, we began our final approach over the Front Range and then the high plains of Denver.

My exhausted and exhilarated mind continued to relive all that had happened and the wonder that we had survived. *Did it really happen? Had I really been in Australia for a week? How did we survive? Did we survive? Am I really alive?*

All this was crashing around in my head as we prepared to land. Even then, feeling supremely tired, achy, dazed, and unsettled, I quietly chuckled to myself, *Wow, so if this is what 'alive' feels like, do I really want this?*

With that thought, my focus turned to what would be awaiting me when I resumed my life in Denver ...

Chapter Fourteen

PICKING UP THE PIECES AFTER UNITED 811
DENVER, COLORADO

EVERYTHING WAS ROUTINE on our final approach into Denver, and when we touched down, my head was spinning. Getting my second wind, my spirits soared as we taxied to the jetway. Deplaning and walking up the jetway, there appeared to be some small crowd and commotion at the doorway, with people and TV cameras jostling to position themselves. Well, I figured it should be easy to step around that ruckus to get to my family, certain that an LA celebrity or sports figure was on board, coming to Colorado to ski or for some sporting event.

Imagine my surprise when walking through the doorway, the crowd turned and began clapping and cheering.

That's when it hit me—this crowd was here for me!

The news teams' lights clicked on, their cameras began whirring, TV news people with microphones, newspaper reporters, and such each clamored to greet me. The other passengers and their companions slowed down or stopped to turn around to watch the activity as my family, friends, coworkers, and loved ones surrounded me, hugging, laughing, crying, patting me on the back, cheering, and all talking at the same time.

When I deplaned, I was exhausted, jet lagged, and numb. How swiftly that changed to feeling beyond joyful just to see everyone. My eyes searched the crowd and found my parents being gently nudged front and center. In the sea of faces, there was my dad, with a huge smile and outstretched arms. Going straight to him, he made a funny comment in my ear and just held me tightly. I could not, nor did I ever want to, let go of him. Dad turned so Mother-Vic could step up, and she also held on to me for a long hug. Looking at Mother-Vic's happy face, and then looking up at Dad's big, strong arm around me and his beaming smile, I knew then I was alive. And home.

Energized by the welcoming chaos at the airport, I wanted to be sure to say hello and speak with every single person who made an effort to greet me.

The boarding area eventually cleared out, and we were ready to head home. Little did I know, there was even more celebrating to follow. Mark and my family spent a great deal of time and energy putting together a grand surprise welcome party at home—everybody, including the local news and TV stations were invited.

In preparation for this surprise party, Mark, Mother-Vic, Dad, Marilyn, Madge, and her two kids, Rachel and Corey, created funny, personal, homemade signs and banners, which they displayed all over the inside and outside of the house.

When our airport greeting party arrived at the house, there were many other cars already parked all along the street. Walking into the house, awaiting us was another heartwarming moment. Here was a house full of friends who waited there as they were unable to be at the airport, and clearly, this group had enjoyed a significant head start kicking off the celebration.

With much more hugging, laughter, food, and beverages, the lower level family room bar area quickly became party central for most of the gang, relegating the TV film crew to set up elsewhere on the main floor to conduct interviews.

Our good-sized house would, in a normal situation, muffle moderate noise in the lower party level, so it would not be heard on the main floor. The commotion from this rowdy group, cheering, making toasts, singing, and dancing, along with the boisterous conversations in the party area, could be heard in the news report videos that were being recorded on the main floor.

My relief to finally and really be home, together with the genuine astonishment at my airport greeting, felt good. After the very stressful time away, and even as tired as I was, to be in the midst of all the celebrations with my family and best friends?

Greatest feeling ever.

March, 1989. Stapleton Airport. My Dad greeting me when I returned from Sydney.

Chapter
Fifteen

MANY SIGNIFICANT CHANGES occurred in my life in the twelve to fourteen months following my return from Australia.

Major national TV and radio programs reached out for interviews resulting in appearances on *Oprah, Turning Point, Hard Copy, Angels II Beyond the Light, Montel Williams, Maury Povich, I Survived a Disaster,* and *It's a Miracle.* Being flown around the country to meet with people like Oprah and her exceptionally talented staff was a totally new experience. A limo met me at O'Hare International Airport in Chicago and whisked me away to a luxury hotel, where I was checked in and given a two-story penthouse suite, food vouchers, and instructions to be ready for the limo pick-up the next day. The following morning, after breakfast, I was whisked off to the studio for makeup and meeting other guests. This was Oprah's second season, and at that time, she chose not to meet guests prior to the show so the conversations would be spontaneous. I remember she was wearing her well-known enormous diamond earrings, and I could hardly take my eyes off them; they were so extraordinary. There were also features in magazines, plus TV and radio appearances in Europe and Australia.

Due to the publicity created by the extensive newspaper and media coverage, strangers felt comfortable approaching me in public boldly asking, "Hey, weren't you on that United flight? I didn't know you had a relative in Tulsa. My brother lives there too." Or people would stare, place their hand over their mouth, and then clearly talk about me with their companions, whispering, "Look over there! No, *there*. That's the lady that was on that flight." Often, I was so tempted to turn to face them, "Hey, I can *hear* you!"

This happened in grocery stores, drugstores, elevators, airports, and department stores. I went from "shut up and stay in the background" to being thrust to front and center stage. It was very new to me, and it was uncomfortable.

Up to this incident, my life evolved from being a happy, outgoing young lady to me being consistently reminded of "my place" and told while in public to "keep your mouth shut because nobody wants to hear what you have to say."

Suddenly, people were lining up to talk to me, talk about me, or ask questions and then listen to what I had to say. That intense and often unwanted attention became another catalyst for the new shift in me.

Within days of my return, United Airlines offered mental health counseling. Randy, my travel agency employer and friend, knew I often played hurt, meaning no matter what I was going through, I would still show up and get the job done.

I poo-pooed the thought of mental health assistance because my mantra at this point was, "I'm fine. Really."

However, Randy strongly suggested I accept the offer before my next scheduled travel assignment in approximately six weeks.

Randy was aware that there was much going on in my emotional life, so this newly added stress and adjustments from the incident likely meant that while I was quietly licking my wounds, I would present a solid front and soldier on.

He firmly believed that counseling would be good not only for the airline incident but just a darn good idea in general. Randy also suggested he would need to see a clean bill of health from a mental health professional before authorizing my participation in the next travel assignment.

Knowing how Randy really cared for and looked after his staff, it made sense that if he was that adamant about this treatment helping me, I would agree to it.

As much as I pushed back on receiving any mental health assistance, my emotions were totally scrambled. Each day was a challenge as I worked to keep my emotional state under control and to present an "I'm OK" front to family, friends, and coworkers.

Every day, my thoughts would drift to who-knew-where, so my attention span was all over the place. My extreme fatigue, confusion, sadness, survivor guilt, insomnia, feeling of being stuck, loss of appetite, and loss of interest in mostly everything created additional daily concerns.

I was simply feeling "lost," and my choice to self-medicate was the only resolution that took the edge off all my internal imbalances, put a rein on my brain, and kept me from going over the ledge.

My conviction that simply getting back on the horse would help me resume life as a normal, functioning person was proving far more difficult than I ever imagined. Plus, I desperately wanted to understand what I was to do, or could do, with this "new" me.

During my first one-hour mental health appointment, the mental health professional asked me to tell him the story of United 811. Then he asked me to repeat the story, then repeat it again. My frustration with him was that I knew what happened—what I needed from him was to help me understand what to do with it. This professional and I did not click.

Advising United of the misconnect with this mental health professional, they sent me to a second mental health professional, where we experienced the same scenario. All those two professionals wanted me to do was repeat and repeat the story, with no "plan" in their treatment picture.

It seemed to me they were encouraging me to wallow around in the look-what-happened-to-me, poor-me aspects of the event, when I knew my best course of action was to find someone to help me understand what was possible with this "new" me who rose up and emerged from the ashes of this incident.

At one of my appointments, the mental health professional mentioned a list of ten potentially life-changing experiences that, should a person experience any one of these events, they were likely a candidate for therapy. Within thirteen months of United 811, I had experienced seven of the ten, and I was spiraling downward.

DIVORCE: Mark and I divorced.

MAJOR MOVE: I moved out of our home to a small condo.

LOSING A PET: On the one-year anniversary of United 811, February 24, 1990, we euthanized Lucy, our big, goofy, and loveable Newfie. She had developed sudden onset lymphatic cancer.

LOSING A PARENT: Shortly after losing Lucy, on

March 5, 1990, my dad suffered a massive heart attack and did not survive heart surgery.

JOB CHANGE: I changed job positions within my company.

LOSING A FAMILY MEMBER: We lost a relative on Mark's side of the family.

TRAUMATIC INCIDENT: Oh, and that United 811 thing ...

Even with all these issues bearing down on me, I deeply felt and recognized I was no victim; I was a survivor, and what I needed was a professional to help me understand what to do with that. I could not grasp why that was so hard for them to comprehend.

Having vetoed the first two counselors, I was braced for the third professional. Upon our introductions, with little conversation or story disclosure from me, his immediate solution was to prescribe three different doses of anxiety medication. One prescription was for "small" anxiety issues, a slightly stronger prescription was for "mild" anxiety issues, and there was a big gun prescription for those "tough" days.

He leaned across his desk to hand me the three prescriptions while he was jabbering on about why these meds made sense. Watching all this from a disassociated, third-party perspective in my brain, it was like watching a scene from a bad movie. My mind was incredulous at his "treatment and treatment options."

As he held the prescription forms out to me, I could

not believe what was happening. Slowly, I became angry and recognized that outward anger was a new response from me, and that was good. Could it be that I was about to speak up in my own defense?

Sitting across his desk from him, I subtly shook my head, certain my look of disgust was clearly showing. Then, in no uncertain terms, I listened to myself interrupt his self-serving speech to explain that after he heard my very brief introduction, he had not even asked, and therefore, had no idea about my usual coping mechanisms. That crap he was peddling for "anxiety"? If I so chose to continue a self-medicating path, I could do far better securing stronger "anxiety medication" on my own. So no, thank you.

Now, in the past, I would have wholeheartedly agreed with his treatment options, snatched those prescriptions out of his hand, and been out the door. That day, it was me taking a stand when I said my piece, standing up and walking out his door, never looking back.

Still sitting in my car in his parking lot, another piece of my personal puzzle had just become clearer—I knew full well that the high levels of medication he wanted to prescribe was no longer the easy way or the stock answer for the "new" me.

The clock was still ticking, and I was only a couple of weeks away from the next travel assignment.

I needed to sort out my options, in order to be declared "ready" to escort a group of clients to St. Thomas, a popular Caribbean destination for our groups and a locale where I often worked. I was frustrated that once I finally and reluctantly agreed to accept mental health assistance, the absence of help was sorely lacking. *So, now that I see I do want help, where do I turn?*

My thoughts turned to Sandi, my good friend and meditation teacher. She answered my call, chuckling in her deep, soothing voice that she had been waiting to hear from me.

A very busy, world-renowned meditation teacher, Sandi found the time to help me augment techniques to relax and find my calm during times of great stress and anxiety. She taught me methods to get out of my own way, which allowed me to see and better understand the big picture when things became muddled in my brain. She showed me how to ground and connect, versus feeling like a lost-in-space character. We worked together to head-on address stresses—one of which was my survivor guilt issues as it related to the seat mix-up and the man in seat 9F.

When this distinguished gentleman refused to give up this duplicate booked seat, I simply found another seat. Because of our choices in that perfectly normal airline/travel moment, I survived, and he did not. *Now, what do I do with that?*

Via meditation, Sandi helped me connect with those nine souls, and then I felt confident they were all right. Together, we explored many facets of the incident, the details surrounding the event, and the ways the experience affected my life.

We agreed that I knew what happened in a big picture sort of way. However, my burning question was, due to the unusual circumstances of the duplicate seat booking, what was I supposed to do with all my emotions tied to that?

What if this gentleman had moved when I showed him my boarding pass, or what if I had arrived at the seat first and, like him, chose to stay put?

Is it bad I am so grateful to be alive? Does that make me a horrible person? I simply didn't know what to do with the endless survivor's guilt over this seating situation.

I deeply and personally felt the loss his family likely experienced and hoped they somehow learned that in his final moments, he was happy and enjoying a beverage and conversation with his seatmate, certain he was not aware what happened to him. It was that sudden.

There were many dark days when I was so conflicted, I wondered if God made a mistake. Maybe it was me that should've been the one to go since I was regularly told I was too stupid to exist and I did not amount to anything.

My saving grace was Sandi. She was the only one who understood my desire and willingness to deeply explore how I coped with this guilt as I moved forward. Sandi helped me understand it is up to me whether I chose to make this a helpful, motivating, life-changing event, or turn it into a drama filled crutch-like, life-stalling event. Victim or survivor?

When I was ready to allow it, she helped me recognize that there are no mistakes—that as I continued to wake up and clarify the dark aspects of the event, I could proceed to live my life in a way that both honored this gentleman's sacrifice and the new "me" who was born from it.

And that was important because so often since United 811, people ask in anger or frustration, "Why does God let bad things happen? Why did you survive and nine others perished?"

Yes. Unfortunately, heartbreaking, terrifying things do happen.

Enormous, gut-wrenching experiences and great losses of a child, spouse, family member, pet, or friend. Think of any of the horrible natural disasters we see. As difficult as it may be to believe while grieving, there does come a time when you are able to turn your focus on what you do with that situation versus maintaining your focus only on the loss, your anger, and disappointment.

Here's how that might look: Perhaps you lost a loved one in an armed conflict, an accident or to a terminal illness, and your grief is unimaginable. In your own time, you will someday be ready to move on from the grief and redirect your energies from the anger and loss. Maybe by creating a way to contribute to medical research geared towards that illness. Or maybe fully participating in support groups for others in the throes of their loss, or in a way unique to you that satisfies you. The bottom line is you choose to make the effort that will honor you and the others involved.

Or you can choose to sit and shake your fist at God. Ask yourself, what happens when you choose that? Nothing. Nothing at all, except you likely go down a very dark rabbit hole, and it's hard to find a positive purpose in that.

Either way you choose, the one thing that never changes is that you still have your loss. The power comes from the choices you make as a result of the loss, and for me, that was my best answer to my question.

Sandi further showed me that it's important that I listen to and trust my own guidance. I will remain confident that no matter what decision I make, I will be able to make it work or I will be able to figure it out, that "no" is a complete sentence, and most importantly, to accept and remember every day that who I was yesterday is not who I am today. And that is OK.

With Sandi's patience and training, plus the help of my family and friends, navigating this difficult time became an enormous learning experience, and my loved ones provided the much-needed help I sought.

Randy also enrolled me in a business stress management seminar as another of his helpful contributions toward my recovery.

My heart was pounding and my hands sweating at registration the day of the seminar. Not knowing what to expect, I entered the event right at the opening introductions and quietly found a seat in the back of the room, tucked into the corner, slightly away from the approximately 100 other attendees.

During the opening remarks, the seminar leader outlined the day's program aimed at business professionals' stress, "Business stress can be problematic, and we'll address that today, but business stress can be managed. For comparison, can you imagine the level and type of stress triggered for the people on that United flight that blew up over Hawaii? Now *that* is real stress."

My jaw dropped, and then a slight smile formed as the people in the room began murmuring "no kidding; can you imagine; glad it wasn't me" comments. Softly chuckling to myself at my welcomed anonymity in the back of the room, I indicated nothing about myself being one of the people he was referencing as an example of *real* stress.

After the seminar, I returned to the office to check in. Sitting at my desk, I began analyzing the helpful information I picked up at the seminar, together with Sandi's healing work and my improved mood at successfully testing snippets of the new "me."

Feeling confident, I walked in to talk with Randy, advising him I was feeling A-OK—that all was good, and let's get on with the next assignment in St. Thomas. He was happy to hear that after my return to work, and with only a few weeks of mental health work, if I was good to go, he was good to send me.

As confident as I felt in that moment, I neglected to

give Randy the complete story. The truth was, I was not entirely "good to go," but damn it, I was GOING TO GO.

I needed to do this next trip to St. Thomas before going back to Australia a few weeks later because in my mind, I was well on my way to being back in the saddle.

Early 1990's. My meditation teacher, Sandi, with one of her beloved miniature donkeys at their Parker, Colorado property.

Chapter Sixteen

DENVER, COLORADO, AND VARIOUS WORK LOCATIONS

GRITTING MY TEETH AS I BOARDED the flight to St. Thomas, I located my requested aisle seat. After United 811, a window view no longer interested me, and most certainly, nothing on the right side of the aircraft. United 811 had given me an enormous open window seat, and I didn't care to sit and look out the window these days.

After a routine flight, the aircraft was on final approach to St. Thomas, and the crew deployed the landing gear. Typically, when landing, there are sounds of grinding and a bump sensation as the landing gear unlocks, rolls into place, and locks for landing.

Seated across the aisle to my right was a young, and obviously newlywed, couple. The young wife gasped and uttered a small shriek when the gear dropped. Her gallant husband immediately placed his arms around her, consoling her, "It's OK, honey. That's a normal sound. Just imagine if you had been on that 747 that the side blew off over Hawaii! We're OK; we're landing soon, and we'll be fine."

Again, little did they know that seated directly across the aisle was someone who knew exactly what they were talking about. Sneaking a sideways glance, I secretly smiled at his bravado and the adoring way she gazed up at him. It was a really sweet moment and another reminder to me of how many people were in some way affected by the United 811 episode—how strangers around me would speak of it, and then right in front of me, apply "something" they took from it and use it in order to complement their lives.

These snippets of United 811 conversations happened often within my earshot. In elevators, people were discussing the airplane that blew up over Hawaii. I overheard conversations in the ladies' room, in restaurants, standing in line for groceries, at the gas station. There was no counting the number of times United 811 was nonchalantly mentioned around me. I watched, listened, and learned from their conversations, every time gratefully recognizing that my survival was truly a gift. Not only for me, but I was then being shown how it affected so many other people. Little did they know, this survivor was still very unsure of herself and how this survival thing was all going to turn out for me.

The St. Thomas trip went off without a hitch, and next up was a return trip to Australia, only six weeks after the United 811 incident. The group and itinerary were very similar to the previous Australian journey. However, this time, rather than traveling alone and early to help set up, traveling with me were approximately sixty-five of our guests who would be joining the larger client group once we all reached Sydney.

Our small group boarded and settled in on the Qantas 747 flying from San Francisco to Honolulu and beyond. Once we settled in, there was a slight delay announced, and we could feel some external jostling of the aircraft. It felt as though the aircraft was being pushed as it slightly swayed left to right after they finished loading baggage.

In my heightened anxiety, I was wondering what that was about as the captain's voice came over the intercom, "Ladies and gentlemen, we'll be delayed a few more minutes here in San Francisco due to a slight problem we are having with our cargo door."

WHAT! WHAT did I just hear? A problem with THE CARGO DOOR! This had to be some sick, cosmic joke—and I wasn't laughing.

At that announcement, my new, more vocal auto response reaction kicked in. Unbuckling from my seat, I headed directly to the first crew member I spotted in the galley.

Then, in no uncertain terms, I advised the cabin crew member that, due to that cargo door announcement, I would not be returning to my seat until I saw and spoke with the captain. I wanted to see the man in charge with the four bars on his sleeve. Now.

Knowing the aircraft couldn't push back from the gate without everyone seated and secure, I held my standing position in the galley. The concerned crew members were asking, "Why all the drama?" Quickly, I explained my recent experience as a passenger on United 811; therefore, I was *not* going to do that again. Further, my responsibilities included sixty-five clients also on board. We would have no problem further delaying this flight while we deplaned this aircraft and retrieved our luggage if someone didn't come down from the cockpit and speak with me.

Puzzled, the purser then asked me if I wanted something to eat. *What!* At that, he immediately backed off, as I must-have given him a "Mother-Vic look of disdain," indicating this conversation was not going to my liking. Again, I advised them I was not moving, and they needed to get that flight crew member for me. Next, I heard, "Well, madam, this is not United; we are Qantas," as if that would rectify everything.

Had I pulled that stunt today, I'd likely still be incarcerated for disrupting a flight. Yes, I was that adamant, and yes, a flight crew member, not the captain, came down and talked with me. My need to look him in the eye, then have him explain everything they had done to ensure the cargo door was indeed checked out and checked off as fully operational and securely locked satisfied me.

Finally convinced, I returned to my seat. I never mentioned to my seatmate clients nor to any of my other sixty-three travel companions why I was talking to the crew or the issue. As our flight departed San Francisco, my seatmates excitedly watched the flight tracker for the start of this adventure.

My heart was racing and my hands sweating as we passed 24,000 feet. Once we achieved cruising altitude, I threw my no-self-medication mindset out the window and reached for a mild sleeping pill, thinking the coincidence of hearing a warning of a potential cargo door problem on nearly the same itinerary as United 811 was too weird. So, if something were to happen, I was not going to witness this one, just let it happen. And happen it did, in a positive way. We had a great time in Australia and an uneventful return flight.

Following this successful second trip to Australia and feeling that I managed two long trips was a huge personal victory for me. These experiences allowed me many opportunities to apply Sandi's guidance to embrace, rather than avoid, the challenges that allowed me to work on regaining my confidence and my voice.

One of my realizations was how my changing life was similar to a swinging pendulum. Having swung so far to the one side of the pendulum of being meek, mild, conditioned to be "small" and insignificant, my life was swinging way to the other side of being recognized, standing up, speaking out, and getting things my way.

Recognizing that side was not the best of me either, my self-talk helped me focus on striving for a more solid middle ground—an ongoing practice to this day and one that I've discovered is a challenge for many people.

IN MARCH, 1990, thirteen months after United 811, I was on my way back to work another group in St. Thomas. Once there, our team immediately began to prepare for our guests' arrival the next day. While we were busy in the conference room, chattering, scurrying around organizing welcome packets, client gifts, and programs, Randy called and asked to speak with me, which was not unusual. He often checked in on our groups or to discuss something going on back at the home office.

Not this time. Picking up the phone, I greeted him with my usual smarty-pants banter. Randy, being my friend, got right to the point. His next words made my world flip upside down and my blood run cold.

"I have bad news—your dad suffered a serious heart attack. He's been rushed to the hospital, and things don't look good. I've made arrangements for you to get the next flight out of St. Thomas to Cedar Rapids."

What did I just hear? *That can't be. My Dad is a Marine, he'll recuperate and then be fine. It's all OK. I just arrived; I don't need to go to Iowa. He'll be fine.*

Randy gently, but firmly, advised me he was not offering a choice of staying on the job or going back to Iowa. The flight arrangements were made.

Hanging up, stunned, I turned to look at the team and told them what I just learned. Having heard myself say it out loud, I excused myself and ran to my room. Sitting on the edge of my bed, shaking, I was frozen in shock and grief. *This could not be happening.*

After frantically repacking everything I'd unpacked less than twelve hours earlier, I hailed a cab and raced back to the airport to catch the flight out of St. Thomas to San Juan, Puerto Rico. Boarding a Chicago nonstop in San Juan, I sat there, numb from the turn of events. I did not know what to expect when I landed in Cedar Rapids. Lost in my thoughts as we were flying somewhere over the Gulf of Mexico, the flight crew announced the movie they would be showing in the cabin was *Dad.*

The date was March 5, 1990. Just days before, on February 24, the one-year anniversary of United 811, I'd put my big, lovable, goofy Newfie dog, Lucy, down. Now this? To say I was not doing well as I tried to process it all was an understatement.

This event with my dad was only one year after United 811, so I was not yet familiar with the unusual circumstances that began to occur around February 24 every year. However, the timing of the movie was another huge wake-up call. My dad survived the emergency heart surgery but did not come out of recovery. He passed as I was watching *Dad* on that San Juan to Chicago flight, tears running down my face.

A FAMILY FRIEND MET me at the gate when we landed in Cedar Rapids very late that evening. Greeting her, I fully expected to hear he was out of surgery and going to be just fine. Leading me away from the crowd, she was still holding me with her arm around my shoulder as she broke the news. She was meeting me as my family was still at the hospital with Mother-Vic because Dad had passed. Gutted with that news, we began gingerly driving the 120 miles from the airport to home in a rapidly brewing and dreadful Iowa ice storm.

Driving late at night in nearly blinding sleet and snow, my head was again struggling to grasp how quickly a routine day can turn around.

Just a few short hours before, I was on a job assignment in sunny St. Thomas. Then, I was driving in the middle of the night in an Iowa ice storm in order to help organize my dad's sudden and entirely unexpected funeral.

Dad had just turned sixty-five a few weeks prior, on February 18. Recently retired, he and Mother-Vic were looking forward to unfettered time together. This was another *what-just-happened* moment, and I was reeling.

By the following morning, the cold, snowy weather and ice made the Iowa roads virtually impassable, which prompted the Iowa governor to declare a state of emergency. Because of the treacherous weather and road conditions, Mark was unable to travel from Denver to Iowa for Dad's services. Even with roads closed, and trees and power lines down due to the storm, 120 people ventured out from all over the state to attend his funeral. With all the details and chores attached to planning these unexpected events in such a short time period, I was constantly cold because I am certain my body was again in a state of shock, plus my only clothes were packed for the tropics.

At the conclusion of Dad's services, Randy again suggested passage back to Denver. Knowing how shaky things were at home and my emotions were again all over the place, I was even more incredibly sad and lost. I decided to leave the ice storm and return to sunny, warm and familiar St. Thomas where I could be by my best grounding mechanism, the ocean. At least there I could be with my good friends on the team in a beautiful Caribbean location and stay busy, or at least distracted, robotically handling the clients' needs.

Shortly after returning from this St. Thomas trip, I was standing at my home kitchen sink, looking out the window while cleaning up after a meal. My legs suddenly became weak, and it felt like my knees were buckling. This was the start of a totally unexpected anxiety attack, and I realized I was about to crumble to the floor.

Grabbing the edge of the counter to steady myself, I began breathing deeply, right as Mark walked behind me to pass through the kitchen. He glanced over his shoulder at me clinging to the counter, then scornfully quipped, "Oh, get over it."

He never broke stride nor stopped to ask what was going on. He did not ask if I was OK, did I need help, or was I about to pass out, nor did he reach out to hold or help me in any way.

Nope. What I got was a snarky, "Oh, get over it."

That was the moment it hit me: I WAS over it.

Still reeling and trying to find my footing after United 811, I wasn't quite ready, or yet strong enough, to throw in the towel on our marriage.

Several weeks later, after another of our clashes, I sat up in bed that night and just watched him sleep, wondering again, *What the hell happened here?* I spent the night going over in my head how this relationship transitioned, what changed, why did it change, could it change again, only this time for the better? And then, as the night began to fade, I knew what I had to do.

As he awoke to find me sitting up, wide-awake and looking at him, it frankly startled him.

He said something like, "What are you doing?" in his dry and condescending way.

Surprised at the strength and resolve in my voice, I replied, "I need to tell you something. It is now clear to me we are together not because of each of other. We are together in spite of each other. I want a divorce."

While this entire scene was so out of character for me, this unexpected conversation at dawn did not sit well with this man who was so completely in control of everything.

While this moment was sad, difficult, and heartbreaking, making this decision and following through with it probably saved my life.

I knew I needed to stick to my guns for my own sanity and health—to find some peace. And with that stress removed, I could find ways to further clean up my act. I was ready for great change, and I did not want another enormous wake-up call to make sure I would do so.

We finalized our divorce approximately eighteen months after United 811.

Chapter Seventeen

FOLLOWING UNITED 811
FEBRUARY, 1991

TWO YEARS LATER, on February 24, 1991, emotionally growing stronger and somewhat back on track with my life, it felt like this two-year anniversary would be a good time to reflect and celebrate life. And what better way to celebrate than with steak, lobster, and champagne in the bright, sunlit condo I was then renting?

Driving home from work, I was feeling upbeat and looking forward to toasting the past two years. Spotting a newer grocery store I'd never visited, I pulled a sharp turn into the busy parking lot bustling with shoppers picking up last-minute items on their way home from work.

Walking briskly through the door of the unfamiliar store, my thoughts were on this hastily planned, impromptu solo and important celebration.

Hurrying past the front door, I slowed to get my bearings and then hustled straight down the baby food aisle, focused on the Seafood/Meat sign at the back of the store.

From the other direction, a woman in a dark blue uniform was walking just as purposefully and directly toward me. Walking right up to me, she stopped in my path and said, "You're Shari Peterson."

I hesitated and then, "Um, yep. I am."

"I'm Sharol Preston. I was a flight crewmember on United 811."

Boom—everything around me just stopped. I stood motionless in my tracks, my thoughts frozen as all the sights and sounds of the busy store faded away.

Silence.

What had I just heard? Everything in that moment halted and my brain short-circuited because what were the chances?

A few seconds passed as we both simply stood there, looking into each other's eyes while we each processed this. Stunned, I felt myself slowly start to breathe again, the shopping scene around me came back into focus. Suddenly, we were chattering away, catching up on the past two years.

Knowing the tasks facing the flight crew that night, I asked Sharol how she was doing. She shared her experiences and difficult recovery since that night. I was taken aback by her own struggles with the incident, flying again after she took the year off, and how she continued to work on the effects this experience had on her life. I shared some of my story with her as well.

Then it hit me, "Do you know what today is?" Saying nothing, she simply shook her head yes.

Musing and thinking out loud, "Wow, and to think we'd run into each other, today, in the baby food aisle. I don't have kids!"

She again shook her head in agreement. "Me, neither!"

Laughing, I said, "And I've never been in this store before—I just stopped as I was driving by."

She looked at me, wide-eyed, "Me too!"

It was a brief, but poignant, conversation. Sharol was on her way to the airport for work and just stopped for snacks and had to get going. Stunned, we hugged each other and shared words of encouragement. Watching her walk away, it took me a few seconds to gather myself and continue shopping. When I reached home and popped the cork on the champagne, I sat in complete amazement at the day's wonderful gift and this reminder of "How Great Thou Art."

Sharol and I ran into each other again a year later when she was a cabin crew member on a United flight from Denver to Sacramento. God bless her; it was great to see her again, and she kept the champagne flowing our direction during that flight!

Annual serendipitous encounters around February 24 began to happen—often something unusual or life-changing happening to me or someone I knew—both happy and unhappy events ranging from illness, loss of pets, and death to joyful unexpected reconnections and surprise reunions. Every year, these events offer a gentle reminder to reflect on the great miracle of surviving United 811.

Another of the crazy coincidences that continue to happen to me. My Dad nicknamed me "Crash" after United 811 so this "Cash Crash" lottery ticket was a joke gift from my family. Note every single number was either an 8 or an 11 and this winning ticket paid $108.

Chapter Eighteen

WHERE DO I GO FROM HERE?
DENVER, COLORADO

PEOPLE OFTEN MISTAKENLY BELIEVE there was a big payout for me after United 811. That was not the case. While there was a class action suit and many passengers received some form of settlement, this compensation was certainly not a "golden egg." After my divorce from Mark, I used those funds as part of the down payment on my house.

I've often felt growing up with limited funds was a blessing, and it also showed me that people often hold different views of what "abundance" is for them. News flash—true abundance is not necessarily buckets of money; rather "abundance" is more accurately represented as plenty of what you personally cherish.

The most content people I've met generally don't focus on money as their happiness meter. Rather, they recognize their abundance as good friends, good family, and good times—maybe discovering no-cost ways to experience real delight with picnics in beautiful locations, watching the sunsets and sunrises, spending unfettered time with their pets or animals, being creative, and discovering unique ways to bring happiness into their lives.

Being frugal also instilled in me the confidence to tackle things that if I had waited until I could afford to do it, I would never have moved forward. Removing any fear of "lack" allowed me to embrace the unexpected, which then became the adventure. I fell many times, only to pick myself up, dust off, and look at things again. That's what lead me to many of the adventures I experienced.

Randy and I continued working together until August 3, 1998. Following a somewhat complicated restructure and merger with another agency, I elected to resign rather than continue under the new management.

The stars again aligned for me because I was not only getting my life back together, this pause button in my career gave me an opportunity to initiate my plan to take about three months off, totally unwind, then find another fulfilling position, likely in another field. The options were wide open for me!

I spent most days simply puttering in my yard, my garden, or around the house. When relaxing, I often reflected on my nearly two decades in the travel arena and how happy I was in the business. Often smiling as I remembered driving to work, being a dork singing out loud in the car, "I love my job! I love going to my job! I love everything about my job!" Yes, that was all true.

What could I possibly do next that would feed my soul like the travel business? As I transitioned from a busy travel employee to this far slower pace, I realized that without the expenses of a corporate job—business clothes and dry-cleaning bills, gas to get to and from work, many restaurant meals, and happy hours -- I could realize some great savings. Plus, with the returns on my investments, it became apparent to me that with careful budgeting, I could survive not working a full-time position. *Hey, this was about to get fun!*

Talking with a friend, reminiscing about the many decades we had known each other and laughing about some of the crazy, fun people we knew and sharing life's stories, she held up her hand and stopped me, "You sit here with all these fun stories, yet you poo-poo all the crap you've been through. How on Earth you maintain your "Good Ship Lollipop" view of your life is beyond me."

She was right—I do tend to focus on the good times and gloss over the many bumps in the road. I simply chose to view my life as a survivor, not a victim.

She reminded me of not only our great travel adventures but also some of my darker times. She mentioned how unusual that is because many people focus on themselves in the oh, poor-me, my-life-is-a-mess reflection. She asked me, "Why is that?"

This question caught me off guard, and I had to really think about that. First, why did that question catch me so off guard? It then hit me that it was because I have never questioned my attitude. I didn't know any other way to address those dark times. And that goes back to how I was raised.

Apologies if this sounds like a broken record, but as you can see from my earliest memories, when something bad happened, we simply got up, dusted off, and carried on.

We were rarely in an environment where we would just sit in our sorrow and feel sorry for ourselves. Not that any of us didn't lick our wounds in private, but why dwell on the bad when my experience has been there was usually something good, or even better, coming in to take its place?

One tough situation that severely challenged my "Good Ship Lollipop" and where I nearly threw in the towel was a five-year period from about 2005–2010 when every fall, I became deathly ill. Around the end of September and until April or May, I was bedridden with constant headaches and nausea, body aches, and extreme fatigue, and I could not think straight. Getting up in the mornings, I would head straight to the sofa to lay down because I was exhausted, so I often slept seventeen or more hours a day. At night, moving from the sofa to prepare for bed, I was so debilitated, I often chose between brushing my teeth or washing my face, as I just did not have the energy to do both.

Incapacitated, I couldn't work, as I could barely form a coherent thought or sentence. This was becoming an annual fall/winter/spring event and was scaring me.

Every spring, as I was feeling better, I'd think this year I might have kicked it. Then, as fall began to set it, I again sought the help of doctors, specialists, and leading area alternative healing practitioners. Over the five years I suffered and sought help through tests, treatments, and every extensive procedure they thought might help. It cost me over $70,000, and still nobody could tell me what was wrong.

My personal physician eventually and reluctantly offered a terminal diagnosis with a three- to five-year life-span prognosis. Hearing that, I drove home from her office and sat in my house in shock, again facing what was apparently a sure end to my life.

Talking with Cindy Galasso, one of my uncannily accurate alternative healer friends, she disagreed with that terminal diagnosis and was adamant there was poison in my blood and it needed to be removed, but that's all she could see. She could not explain how it got there, what kind of poison, or what to do. But at least I finally had "something"—and it was in my blood.

With that information, I called housing inspector professionals to schedule them to thoroughly check my house for mold or toxic construction materials, something nasty living in the heating ducts, or if they could uncover anything in my living environment that would make me this sick. They found nothing toxic or life-threatening, so the inspector was surprised that his glowing report upset me.

Within a few days of my terminal diagnosis, I knew I had to get to my personal safety net, the ocean, to get my bearings. With my little sister, Madge, and her daughter, Rachel, we landed in San Diego, where we immediately headed to the beach. Plopping down onto the sand, watching the ocean, I could feel myself returning to normal, and then, I had to face the facts of my recent diagnosis

By the next day, I was feeling considerably better. Chatting with one of the lifeguards, he was intrigued with my health story and asked if he could check my blood oxygen levels. The readings were surprisingly improved in such a short time (less than twenty-four hours), so I thought, "Perfect. I guess I need to move here and die on the beach after all."

I returned home after a few days to meet the local utility company representative who was scheduled do a courtesy check of my home and appliances for their efficiency.

The worker was there a short time, then came around the corner of the living room to where I was curled up on the sofa. Not saying anything, he paused for several seconds, scratching his head with a puzzled look, "Um, are you experiencing any headaches, fatigue, aches, and confusion?"

Snapping up into a sitting position, I shouted, "YES! Why do you ask?"

Still frowning, he continued, "Well, you have a carbon monoxide leak coming from your water heater. I can see when it was installed, and the coupling was incorrectly attached. Because the coupling is not matched up, the carbon monoxide is continually overflowing from that lousy connection, and it needs to be fixed immediately."

Even though I had a carbon monoxide detector, it was located by my bed so I could hear it go off, rather than near the water heater so it could detect any issues. *Duh.* It never sounded an alarm.

Because I always slept with the bedroom window above my head slightly cracked open except in extreme winter weather, he said that slight amount of fresh air directly over my bed likely saved my life.

Even in my foggy brain, this was starting to make perfect sense—that when the days cooled down, I shut most of the house windows and that trapped the gas. In the spring, I loved the fresh air, so I opened up the house at every opportunity. That fall close down/spring open up house schedule perfectly fit the pattern of my distress. Plus, the carbon monoxide enters the bloodstream, and my friend was 100 percent correct—my blood was poisoned.

Within twenty-four hours of the repair, I felt significantly better. Contacting the company that incorrectly installed the water heater to advise them of the issue, they immediately pushed back hard legally. I had no energy to fight for my lost wages or the costs I incurred, and I was disappointed they would not do the right thing for me.

Even today, it is distressing to realize the hundreds of thousands of dollars it cost me financing my medical expenses and paying my business and living expenses with zero income for over five years—not to mention the time I lost in extreme stress and in that brain fog.

In the midst of the carbon monoxide haze years, I was cleaning my bathroom using strong chemicals. When the bleach I had in the tub mixed with the ammonia I'd sprayed on the walls, the immediate reaction created chlorine gas, which knocked me back.

Feeling I had been physically pushed back, I fell out of the bathroom onto the bedroom floor, my lungs felt like they were melting. Picture hot bacon grease poured on a Styrofoam plate. That's what my lungs felt like.

Having no clue what just happened, I lay on the floor where I landed, stunned and running a mental check on my body. *Did I break anything when I fell? What the hell is going on with my breathing—that ain't right.*

Not one to leave a job undone, I sat up and waited a few more minutes before getting up. Steadying myself, then covering my nose and mouth with the sweatshirt sleeve on my left arm and gagging, I went back in to quickly finish up. The bathroom window was open, but I could feel myself reacting to whatever was going on and stumbled out of the bathroom again and crumbled back on the floor of my bedroom to try and get my bearings.

Dumb, dumb, dumb . . . but again, I had to get back on that horse and finish the project!

Feeling like I had been kicked in the chest, I moved to the sofa and lay down, waiting for this horrible feeling in my lungs to just go away.

After about a week of little improvement, I convinced myself to check in with Poison Control, as this was just "not right." The operator heard what I had done, interrupted me, and strongly urged me to get to the doctor. It had already been a week, so my response of, "Oh, I'll get on that tomorrow," was met with, "No, you get to the ER now."

With the insistence in her voice, I promptly drove myself to the ER. The staff couldn't believe I mixed those two chemicals and created and inhaled chlorine gas, then went back into the room and survived! Silly me, I asked, "What? I didn't know you can't mix those together, and what is chlorine gas?" The nurse slowly lifted her head, looking at me, "Um, the gas they used to kill people in WWI." *What?*

That was a sobering doctors visit, for sure. The next morning, the gal at Poison Control called to check on me; she was that concerned. I'm as recovered as I can be, but there is some permanent lung damage, so exerting myself is something I needed to monitor.

As my friend and I talked about my experiences since United 811 and my good attitude and determination to work through them, we shared additional significant bumpy patches. These incidents felt to me like clearing the slate for whatever new and better things would be coming into my life.

My slate clearing also included three cancer scares, a third divorce, and a "friend" who scammed me and several in our group out of large sums of money—me, personally, for $50,000, along with a business deal in Southern California that ended up costing me hundreds of thousands of dollars, plus attorney fees.

I was reeling as my health, my personal life, and my finances all blew up, so it opened me up to the opportunity for another new experience—a nervous breakdown.

This was all just too much, and I began to withdraw, not sleeping, not eating, drinking way too much, and self-medicating. My high blood pressure was out of control, and I just felt awful.

Waking up one night, my insides felt like they were going to explode. My head was pounding, and I could feel every beat of my heart in my entire body. The feelings were so unusual and alarming, I got up and took my blood pressure. The reading was 220/110. That had to be a mistake, so I took it again—same thing.

Calling my doctor's service, in seconds, I was told to get to the ER. Gathering my wits, I explained I would change my clothes and drive over as soon as I could. The operator said, "NO, you are in a critical situation. Call 911."

Hanging up, taking a deep breath, I called 911 and explained my condition. They advised me to hang up, unlock the front door, sit in a chair near the door, and wait for help.

With all this sudden sense of urgency from the 911 dispatcher, I was feeling scared and wondering what was going on. The EMTs arrived within minutes, loaded me on the stretcher and I was off on my first ambulance ride. The EMTs worked to get my blood pressure down on the short ride, and once I was in the hospital, their ER team kept pumping me with drugs and monitoring my readings. Nothing was working.

It didn't help that I could hear what was going on with the patient on the other side of the curtain. An elderly woman had come in with low blood pressure. She didn't survive and I overheard her entire experience so that didn't help my high blood pressure.

After several hours, the medical team finally got my symptoms under control, and I was OK to be released. Looking at the time, it was going on five a.m. The hospital staff asked if they could call someone to collect me. I assured them I would be OK if they could just call me a cab.

After all that stress, sitting alone in the back of that dark cab in my sweats looking at the bandage on my hand where the IV had been, tears began slowly running down my cheeks as I thought, *This is getting to be just too much* ...

DR. CHRIS ANDERSON is a trusted family friend and

a terrific alternative healer. We met to discuss this latest health development, and she ran some blood tests. Calling me back after she received the results, her stern first words when I answered the phone were, "I don't know how you are even functioning; your organs are shutting down."

She immediately put together a program for my body type and gave me things to watch for. She and I had a very frank conversation about next steps if this didn't turn around in thirty days. Anyway, as is my nature, I was diligent and followed everything to the letter. I was determined to get a handle on all this. The thirty-day results exceeded Dr. Chris' expectations, and I was finally on the road to improvement. Dr. Chris, with her calm, steady, no-nonsense care and genuine concern for my well-being, likely saved my life.

After years of everything crashing around me, I was facing an entirely new environment and life. No longer could I enjoy financially carefree days, traveling on a whim, fine dining, and spontaneous adventures. It was time to sweep up and sort out what was left of my life.

That was a very scary place to be at sixty-plus years old. Again, I was grateful for knowing how to rearrange my life to fit my budget and even more grateful for my experience with Plan Bs.

Chapter Nineteen

MY EPIPHANY

EPIPHANY: A visceral understanding of something you already knew.

Recognizing all these changes as an opportunity to create a different version of my life, I sat down and pondered loss.

Why do so many people feel loss is sad and the end of something; why do they shake their fists at the sky and rail against God? What if a loss was actually the start of something, and could eventually make you stronger? After all, when the door closes, turn around and look for the open window, right?

To really delve into this, I cleared an entire weekend and determined this time would allow me to sequester myself in my house and sort through some nagging mental and emotional questions.

My first step was to define "loss" and what it meant to me. How did I feel when I faced loss, and why did I feel that way?

My dad's voice came to me with this reminder, "Nobody ever packed a suitcase for their own funeral." The first time I heard him say that, I was a small child, and the visual struck me as funny. A dead person with a suitcase taking their stuff to their grave. That's dumb.

Thinking of his statement as an adult, I thought about all the things I thought were so important to me as a child—a piece of favorite clothing, a toy, or a pet. It dawned on me that everything we ever achieve or have, we will eventually lose. Because it ain't going in the suitcase and with me to the grave!

There is nothing, or "no thing," we keep forever. Our physical possessions will all leave us. A favorite watch or jewelry? Accidently left it at the gym. Money? We earn and spend it. Clothes, cars, electronic devices, sporting equipment, pets, and people? They will all leave us due to life changes or even death.

Why do we covet stuff? Because the truth is we do not take anything with us all the way through this life or after this life. Things are simply loaned to us during our time here on Earth. What we choose to do with them, or the value we place on them, is totally on us.

Beginning that Friday night, I slowly looked at

everything I had in my house and in my world. Taking my time, I would enter a room, pick up an object, spend some time looking at it, and ask myself what this would do for me and what this new life I was going to have would look like.

I looked at each room in my house, the furnishings, my vast collection of books, recent and old photographs, my kitchen pots and pans. In the garage, I stood with my car, my lawnmower, my garden tools. Then back into my house and out the large sliding doors into my enormous, lush backyard. Back to my favorite chair where I contemplated my job, my relationships, my interests. I realized each object I held in my attention generated a feeling or strong emotion. Happy and cheerful or sad and mournful were the two most consistent visceral responses.

Taking my time, I let my mind wander to contemplate whatever emotion each object created. Then maybe I'd go back to rethink another item. By Sunday, it was clear to me—the object would always be, or eventually be, a loss, but the emotion it created was with me forever.

If I had to leave *right now* and take only important items with me, all that would qualify would be myself and my pets, which at that time were my beautiful, loving, and goofy Golden Retriever, Brandy, my alpha cat, Ocho, two parakeets, and a tank of fish.

By late that Sunday afternoon, I was nearly giddy with relief and fully engaged with the accompanying feelings of liberation and excitement at the success of this personal retreat.

I was satisfied I truly understood the meaning of "detachment" for me—that is the ability for me to fully appreciate and care for whatever is in my life in that moment. And when it goes away, I will be able to understand the natural grieving process, knowing those feelings are real and will pass. Plus, this change also flings open the door for the next thing when I am ready to welcome it into my world.

This epiphany allowed me to fully turn my attention to the future and stop looking at these experiences as great losses. My new goal was to apply my experiences and energy toward opportunities that allowed me to contribute to projects and do it on my schedule. To achieve that would be my new and authentic abundance.

I began discovering and exploring amusing projects that often allowed me to work from home, were fun, and fed my soul.

Some of the projects were helping my neighbor in her high-end interior design business, assisting a successful speaker and author as her marketing manager, and working retail over the holidays in some of the local upscale boutiques. One extremely satisfying position was helping my friends who owned a popular, premier travel agency and travel store selling guidebooks, luggage, travel clothing, and all the little travel items that make life easier on the road. It kept me plugged into travel and the interesting people exploring exotic locations. I was able to help them put together items that would make their trip much easier.

Recognizing my personal satisfaction when I am able to help people, I researched and discovered a new (at that time) vocation termed "life coach." I immediately enrolled in a one-week, well-rated, accredited life coach training program in Del Mar, California, but I soon discovered the instructor and I had very different views on how to approach life issues. She flunked me. I was the only attendee who did not successfully complete her program.

That "failure" did not phase me in the least because from what I observed of her procedures, nobody was going to better understand their lives using the complicated nonsense, dare I say, bullshit, she was sharing.

Interestingly, over the next few months, every single student in that class contacted me for assistance with their own issues. Sorting through their obstacles and question marks in their lives, many varied resolutions and new ways of thinking were reached using my own processes. These successes showed me it was even more apparent I didn't need that piece of paper from her to help initiate positive change with people.

From those productive experiences with my fellow class attendees and their referrals, I also began working with people in person at my home and through a joint office with other alternative healing practitioners. The coaching evolved into working with couples and eventually officiating weddings.

During the fifteen-plus years of officiating weddings, funerals, and birthing celebrations, I met many unique couples and vendors. One vendor owned a large, local dove release business, and we would see each other at various wedding or funeral venues. One day, he mentioned how he had so much business, he needed to find help—someone who could effortlessly handle a wild animal and publicly speak at the same time. So, dove releases became another of my fun, groovy undertakings.

He taught me how to reach into the carrier to remove the bird or birds, depending on the situation and grip them so they would remain still and not fight me, which would be a mess if they were squawking and flapping during a service, then look around to ensure there were no predators in the sky before gently releasing them into the air—all the while making a presentation of some sort, again depending on the type of ceremony.

It sounded easy, but he had me come to his facility to practice, and then he sent me home with crates of doves to practice on my own.

Knowing this was right up Mother-Vic's alley, I called and told her what I was doing. She insisted I come to her house to practice. By the time I arrived, she had set up lawn chairs in her front yard, invited some neighbors over, and was mixing cocktails for everybody.

My car back seat was filled with crates of birds, so we removed them, and I got to work. Slowly reaching in the crate, I caught one. Then I had to catch the second one with only one hand and look smooth doing it. Success!

I positioned them, said a few words, and released them, but this first one didn't go well because it is natural to lift your hands up and toward each other, so I ended up pushing them into each other as they took off. Nothing grace-filled about that first launch.

Mother-Vic started laughing so hard I thought she was going to spit out her vodka tonic. *OK, note to self, release them AWAY from each other.*

The birds were fascinating with their homing instincts, and I learned a lot during this brief six-month endeavor. The owner eventually cut back on his engagements, allowing him to handle everything himself. We still saw each other at events, and I still enjoy watching dove releases.

Working through the life stresses of the people I coached, I recognized the financial challenges many were experiencing and decided to organize a financial education company to help people understand the financial system and make better decisions. That evolved into a small insurance agency and then into a branch of a reverse mortgage company.

I was coaching a client one day who mentioned her ongoing frustration with her life. She was no longer in therapy, so she announced she was going to let me sort it out for her.

Whoa, whoa, whoa.

Let *me* sort it out *for* her? That lead to a long discussion that I was not going to sort anything out *for* her; my goal was to help her discover ways she could better manage her own life.

She pushed back hard, and on that note, I finished up with all my current clients, effectively closing my office. I was through working with that victim, poor-me, make-it-better-for-me mindset of stubborn people who refused to do the work. I realized the large number of people I met who felt powerless and confused with their lives engaged so-called professionals for help. Then, they again handed their power over to that person. They learn nothing and gain nothing by always expecting someone else to give them their answers; what they need is help in ways to *discover* their own answers.

There are those who are comfortable in the victim mindset. It keeps their life exciting, gets them a lot of attention, and they fear having to be in charge of their own life. It is much easier for them to point fingers at everybody else, and then repeat their version of the story of all those who make it tough for them to live well. Yup, I was done with that.

I took other part-time jobs because they were physically challenging, and I thought it was a bonus. Why not be paid to enjoy a little workout?

A must-have for me is a flexible schedule, and that led me to filling orders in warehouses during their busy days or working in the concession stands at Coors Field during baseball season.

One of my favorite projects is helping the ticketing staff at the National Western Stock Show pull that event together every year. The Stock Show is such a grand, local Denver tradition and attracts the nicest attendees. The staff that gathers every year for this sixteen-day event are some unique personalities.

During the summers, I volunteer and work with my friends who own what is considered the second quirkiest thing to do in Colorado—the Sasquatch Outpost and Museum in the beautiful mountain community of Bailey, fifty miles west of Denver. The drive out of the city and into the mountains absolutely feeds my soul, and I always feel any tension and stress just drift away as I motor up there. The beautiful scenery and the fresh air, and when I arrive, all the unique regulars and visitors that drop by to see us at the store are a real treat.

Among all of this activity, I still find time to take advantage of every travel opportunity that comes my way, from flying to see friends and family or enjoying one of my favorite things, road trips! The western states are so wide open and beautiful. Plus, there is so much to see. I spent some time exploring Route 66 one summer. And, of course, my public speaking opportunities. What a great way to allow me to combine my favorite things while managing my own, flexible schedule. I get to travel, meet new people, and help them in some way. Ain't life grand?

Chapter Twenty

THE END?

THERE IS NO "THE END" to my story.

Every day, I ponder the significance of this simple question: "What the hell just happened?" Not only regarding United 811, but also many times throughout a variety of events in my life.

I now view every morning as a new beginning and each day another opportunity to face fears, makes mistakes, take risks, and overcome challenges.

People often ask me why, after thirty years, are you now sharing your story?

Every time I was asked that, I struggled within myself to find a response, until I recognized that not every question has a single answer.

The experiences presented by United 811, and the many incidents that followed, helped me grow in ways that continually teach me new ways to face many daily challenges. I discovered in talking with people about this book and the incident that not one single person has the entire story. I didn't share much during that time because that was just not me.

Also, I realized that people, myself included, often believe life is only good when there are no bumps or challenges. Slowly, I discovered believing or buying into that mind-set seldom supports being happy and present.

That view often opened the door to depression because even when you may feel defeated, in truth, your life is probably normal and good. It is just not perfect!

That self-imposed defeated belief often morphs into you-are-not-enough false conclusions and thought patterns. From there emerges a victim mentality, where people feel stuck and even believe that all their manufactured drama *is* their true story.

Everybody has bad days; people simply forget those days are not who they really are.

Rather than the poor-me, this-life-is-so-mean-to-me story, look at how different your view and mental state is when you full-on face challenges, which is not to be confused with welcoming them with stardust in your eyes and visions of unicorns dancing on the horizon.

Every day, every moment, be authentic, present, patient, and kind with yourself. Recognize all this, and by being brave, you can discover the courage and confidence to turn and face life's obstacles, rather than run from, ignore, or even invent a far-fetched story.

You will recognize that while some challenges will be managed in a short time, some may take years to recognize, understand, and manage. That's just life!

What a great discovery, when you understand the good in life comes from what you learn through the challenges and then what you do with them. Challenges and being truly grateful for their outcomes, give us the opportunity to grow stronger, smarter, and even more resilient.

Remember the chick breaking out of the egg is fighting to break the shell naturally. That fight makes the chick tough enough to successfully work its way out, and then has a far better chance for survival in the real world.

Nature teaches and shows us how all creatures grow stronger because of their fight in difficult conditions. Those natural predicaments are what allow us the opportunity to step up, change, break free, and then come out the other side strong and powerful.

It is what you DO with the challenge you face that creates you and the quality of your life. After all, a smooth sea never made a skilled sailor!

Will you choose to spend your time and energy *reacting* to your life and treading water? Or would you rather focus on *creating* your life and then going with the flow?

Reminding yourself there are no right or wrong

decisions, remember that your choices set you on a path to travel the long way or the short way. Either way, you will get to where you need to be, in the time frame that is perfect for you.

I had to face many demons when my second marriage ended as I again looked into the face of defeat and loss of self. In this case, I had been repeatedly told I was "too stupid to live on my own" and that I could "never manage a place of my own" and that "I don't know what to do about anything" and that "who would want to be with you because they will have to financially support you. You clearly cannot support yourself" and so on. It was time to figure out why I made my partner choices and my part in each of these past relationships.

We've all heard, "Youth is wasted on the young." Well, the younger me loved the fun, life of the party, bad boys. Because they were such great fun, why wouldn't I want to party, laugh, and play for the rest of my life?

But I also had to face why it was I thought that person would make a good life partner. I simply didn't have the life experiences to know that was where I should focus. I was familiar with dating and hanging out and having fun, but nowhere in my experience were there adult challenges like mortgages, insurance, adult jobs. I often mused and joked with Mother-Vic that it was their fault I was divorced because they made marriage look easy and fun.

In my search, I recall one spontaneous conversation with an insightful, young gal. She had a wonderful, fun boyfriend all through college. Nearing the end of their senior year, when their close-knit circle of college friends were getting engaged, she broke up with him. He was planning to propose, and he was devastated. She told him he was great fun and a great boyfriend through college, but she could not see him as husband and father material in a real life.

She moved on, married a wonderful man, and was enjoying life. She found she was also correct about her college boyfriend. While a great guy, after graduation he attempted to settle down and prove her wrong. Struggling with the "grown-up lifestyle," he eventually happily reverted to his life of arrested development. Had they married, the joy and common interests they shared in college would have been the very same things that would have caused tension between them later on. Their different lifestyles and goals worked as "daters" but would never have worked as a marriage.

I've had many conversations with young couples, and I often ask, "Why do you want to marry this person?" If their answer was, "We're in love," while appropriate and sweet, that's probably not going to go as well as when the answer was, "Because she laughs every time I absent-mindedly put the milk in the cupboard and cereal in the fridge" or "He washes and fills my car every Saturday morning." One couple set every Friday night aside for just them to create a new cocktail to enjoy as they un-plugged all devices until Saturday morning. Then they sipped, talked, and tried the new dinner recipe one of them selected—things friends do together.

The very things that many young couples found attractive about each other were, years later, often the same traits that drove a wedge into the relationship.

"He's so charming and so much fun at parties" became "he's a big flirt."

"She's so together and focused regarding work and finances" became "she's uptight, no fun, and a miser."

"He's so generous and loving" became "he's such a pushover to his friends."

"She's so easygoing, never gets mad, and we never fight" became "she is wishy-washy, has no opinion, and I don't know where she stands on any topic."

Couples who mainly focus on having fun think they are in love, and so they marry. Unexpectedly the dating fun/common ground turns into the adult world, and then it isn't "fun" anymore.

I often see couples today look for the fun and love (having), versus seeking a partner and friend (being). Being friends is the most important component to also being in love for a long-term partnership. Find someone who you trust will have your back and allow you to have theirs. The love "feeling" can be fickle and fleeting. However, loving friends are the solid base for a dependable, genuine, long-term relationship.

ANOTHER REVELATION for me was people who wax

on and on about positive thinking and suggest many practices to manifest or create a version of abundance. However, for me, this idea of creating abundance is far more extensive than simply "thinking" it into being.

Taking my dad's cue, I suggest people meditate and fully understand the situation regarding what they choose to manifest. Will that "thing" they think they want really satisfy them, or have they simply convinced themselves it will?

To find out, meditate on the desire; ask if this desire is about having something or about being something. Which one will truly satisfy the authentic you? Once you achieve the thing, what will you do with it?

When you are clear on those questions, define the challenges blocking you from this desire. What steps do you need to take to create a clear path to allow this desire to come into your life?

Once you are satisfied you have gathered and understand that information, you can get to work and confidently remove those roadblocks. Roadblocks you have both identified and those that pop up along that way— which incidentally, often become the great adventure.

You want a boat? Duh—You'll need to move near water. You may need to take classes on how to sail or work part time jobs to build up the funds to be able to afford a move to a location. Maybe a job in the boating industry to get familiar with the lifestyle and determine the best boat for you. Plus are you prepared for the responsibilities of fuel, insurance, dock fees, and so forth.

As you work through these issues to achieve your goal, you will naturally behave in ways that will demonstrate to you this either is not at all what you really desire, or you will become even more motivated about your goal. If it is your true desire, these actions further integrate you into the culture of your goal, in this case, the boating community, and eventually you will achieve it! See, you don't just "think" these things into action, true manifestation is recognizing, then consciously handling the real life obstacles, thus creating the path for the opportunity to come to you.

Here's a way I suggest people better understand this simple process to manifest or create their personal abundance at a natural pace rather than becoming impatient and disillusioned:

Slow down, and think about the universal laws of nature and animals. Animals seem to get through life free of stress by living in the moment. We human animals are the only mammals that worry. We worry about food, shelter, money, family, and more.

Our pets, livestock, animals in the wild, even nature represented as forests or our gardens operate by these universal and irrefutable laws—one of which is they must fight in order to grow. We humans typically believe we don't operate under those same laws; we look for the fast or easy way.

Things flow far smoother when we remember to allow a situation to unfold as we work with it, let go of the stress we create by trying to manipulate the matter.

Often a good reminder for me is the comparison of planting a seed and watching it grow. When I am impatient and wanting something to happen in my time, my reminder to "get real" is a mental image of me sitting in a garden in front of a recently planted seed.

Wanting something to happen "right now" is like digging in the dirt and pulling at that seedling to stretch it or check its roots to make it grow faster.

What have I done? Likely stunted its growth, damaged it, or maybe even killed it. The seed will grow and sprout on its schedule, not mine. And when the seed naturally produces, I am grateful for the bounty.

My part in this metaphor is to either leave it alone and allow it to grow as nature intended, or perhaps care for it by providing the food, water, and support it needs.

My suggestion is to apply this analogy with your own challenges and treat them as a growing experience rather than a poor-me experience.

Another situation that stymies people is recognizing their part in any of their own life difficulties. Rather than pointing fingers at all the people they believe are ruining their life, perhaps it would be more helpful for them to view matters as a puzzle, not a problem:

What is the challenge?

What is my part in this?

Here's the trick—being brutally honest. Am I satisfied with my part in this?

If satisfied with my part in the matter, what can I contribute to improve this?

If not satisfied up to this point with my part, what can I change to then contribute to this situation?

What do I see as the worst things that can happen by my decisions and/or by my next actions?

What do I see as the best things that can happen by my decisions and/or by my next actions?

What do I see happening if I make no changes, no decision?

Total honesty, no matter how painful, is essential as you conduct your review. Rationalizing or sugarcoating to make you feel better will not help you in any way.

Here's an example of rationalizing:

When you have a headache, you automatically take aspirin because you rationalize that will make you feel better. OK, that may work, but when you are honest and *not* rationalizing, we all know the real solution for your headache is "stop drinking tequila."

In this case, you can now see what course of action to take to change the root of the uncomfortable situation, and that changes everything. Or you could stick with your version and choose the temporary solution because that is how you choose to sugarcoat the situation.

It is key to identify and cure the **cause** of the condition rather than put a bandage over it. The bandage only addresses the **result** of the condition.

Also, we often forget to pay attention to that little voice, the one we all have and often ignore. That voice often helps me view things in a different and clearer way which quite often saves my neck!

When I speak of this innate intuition we all have, the majority of the time people light up and say the same thing – "Gosh, you are right! When I listen to my intuition, things do seem to go smoother. When I ignore that voice, things seem to often become a challenge."

ANOTHER OFTEN ASKED question is what changed for me, spiritually, after United 811?

An example of how this incident opened my eyes to infinite possibilities began while talking with Nadene, one of my thirty-plus-year friends from Sandi's meditation class. One of the first times I saw Nadene after the incident, she nonchalantly asked, "Hey, why did you tighten your seat belt?"

Suddenly, that part of the story came crashing back on me as I incredulously and quietly replied, "Because I was told to."

My story had so revolved around the disaster, the drama, the activity around the explosion, and the eventual outcome of the landing, I had lost track of the "why" did I give that seat belt a yank—a simple movement that quite likely saved my life. Had I chosen to ignore or pooh-pooh that one instruction, the outcome for me would have been fatal.

A few days later, Nadene mentioned she was thinking about our conversation. She believed the memory I recovered affected me, so it appeared to be significant and worth exploring.

She suggested I pick up the recent best seller *Ask Your Angels*, written by Alma Daniel, Timothy Wyllie, and Andrew Ramer.

Because I trust Nadene and her incredible insights, I bought and read the book. Then I read it again. And again, highlighting passages, applying the techniques, and it absolutely opened my eyes to the possibilities of ethereal support during this United 811 incident, and even more so in the events that followed it.

In May 1993, I traveled to Boston with my one of my BFFs, Janelle, to visit another of our BFFs, Vicki-Lynn. Vicki-Lynn surprised us with a daylong *"Ask Your Angels"* seminar lead by Alma and Timothy.

Having read their book cover to cover and back again, I could barely contain my delight as I was soon to meet them. The event exceeded my expectations, and at the first break, I thanked them for all the help their book provided me. From that day forward, Alma Daniel and I have stayed in touch, nurtured and continue to enjoy an amazing friendship. Alma is truly one of my angels.

ANOTHER WAY MY SPIRITUALITY changed post United 811 runs parallel to the idea that "not every question has a single answer." Allow me to use water as an example to put into words my spiritual experience.

Imagine that as youngsters, we were told about water and swimming. It was something we should know because water can improve our lives and swimming may even save our lives.

To learn all we can about water, we took classes, read, studied, and researched water. We read about water and swimming, about holding our breath while in water, putting our head under water, moving our arms and legs in a way that will propel us through water, how water can save us or kill us, so we need to know about water.

All this reading and research, and yet, none of these students have ever been in water.

The students have, however, read about water, sat for the tests on water, and passed them with honors. On a paper, showing the high grades, these students are now considered experts and highly qualified to teach others about swimming and water.

Right?

However, one student was pushed into the water, and while this was clearly an unknown challenge, scary, and not that much fun to inhale water and choke, she quickly and naturally learned to swim. From firsthand experience, now she knows far more about water than the book-learned students!

The impetuous student, having fully experienced water now **knows** what happens when you don't hold your breath. This student now **knows** not everybody moves their arms and legs the same way to get through water because some swimmers are really good and fast, others not so much, but she now realizes it isn't how they did it, but that they still got to the other side and didn't drown.

Which student is really understanding water and why?

The student who was pushed in thought she was going to drown, fought to get out of the water, and therefore figured it out. That student may not pass all the written tests on the subject of water. But this student "**knows**" water.

Having experienced United 811 helped me better understand my faith because I no longer have to read about faith to understand it.

"To have faith is to trust yourself to the water. When you swim, you don't grab hold of the water because if you do, you will sink and drown. Instead, you relax and float." —*Philosopher Alan Watts*

When people remain authentic, are truly grateful for what they receive, and are open to celebrate all the wonders surrounding them, lives change and even miracles happen.

EVERYBODY HAS A STORY. What are you doing with yours?

Thirty-plus years after this life-changing event, I continue to explore and learn even more.

I learned acceptance doesn't mean you agree with

something, it means you can accept that it is happening. You need not push back; simply look it over and make good choices with what you have.

I learned I want to be inspired, not lectured.

I learned the meaning of life is to give life meaning.

I learned the best life is a no-excuses life. When experiencing a loss, allow the grieving process before moving forward.

I learned you don't always have to know the answers; it is far more important to know the questions. What you ask and how you ask those questions are far more important.

I learned too many people are not living their dreams because they are living in their fears.

I learned choices I make can help me grow wise rather than growing old.

I learned to fully embrace constructive criticism. When looking at the source of the criticism, the reason for the criticism, the potential outcomes of embracing or ignoring the criticism, I then grow from whatever it is that I take from the criticism.

Imagine what you could do if you knew you could not fail?

Because we never fail, we always succeed. Sometimes, we just don't see it. Take any situation, and some see themselves as victims. Others, in the same scenario, see themselves as survivors and thrive from the experience.

I learned everybody I talked with that was affected

by United 811 had a different and very personal version of the same experience, and I can only share my distant recollection and reflections after 30 years.

If you were one of the people affected by United 811 as a crew member, a first responder, a United employee who assisted on the ground, a passenger or family member, and you want to talk about this incident, I am curious what you experienced and have what you have done since United 811.

Even today, I think of all the people involved and how their lives may have been affected. I would love to hear your stories and express my gratitude for any help or assistance you may have offered me. Some of the smallest courtesies made the biggest impression on me or helped me in ways you cannot imagine, and I thank you.

May 22, 1993, Boston Area. Janelle Sparkman, Authors Timothy Wylie and Alma Daniel, Shari, and Vicki-Lynn Wages. We are meeting Timothy and Alma for the first time at a one day event for their book, "Ask Your Angels." We girls had so much fun with these two!

Reflections

"The cure for anything is salt water: sweat,
tears, or the sea." —*Isak Dinesan*

A Hawaiian sunset on any day is also a mystical and breathtaking experience.

Reclining on the warm sand, late afternoon sunlight warms my face; the colors of the sky morph from bright blue into streaks of reddish golden hues as the sun slowly begins dropping into the endless blue water of the Pacific.

The secluded Kauai beach house sits behind me; the beachside grill sizzles with fresh fish purchased directly off the local fishing boats. Cool early evening breezes blowing in off the ocean create a harmony of rustling palm trees. Savoring a glass of chilled local pineapple wine, I marvel at the sounds and heavenly tropical scents of the surrounding nature and beauty.

Leaning back, my legs outstretched and my fingers playing in the sand, I become mesmerized by the sights and sounds of the waves softly breaking over the sandy beach.

Visiting Hawaii, my thoughts inevitably ponder the important chunks of my past that occurred here, forever changing my life.

I smile and contemplate a lifetime of discoveries, adventure, uncomfortable and scary conditions, times of love and longing. I reflect on my days of unspeakable sorrow, loneliness, disappointment, heartache, and also my years of great freedom, joy, and happiness. Every one of these encounters moved, inspired, comforted, and challenged me in some way.

As my fingers absentmindedly caress and pat the sand, Kealoha's soft, mischievous chuckle and magical presence interrupts my reverie. Welcoming her to my thoughts, a slight giggle escapes me. Her words ring true; my heart is truly happy here, and I do come back to Hawaii.

Softly speaking the Hawaiian words for "living life" ("Ola, Ola)" I raise my glass in a salute to the sea. Watching as the clouds capture the bold colors of the final scattering rays, I blissfully toast another fine Hawaiian day.

Aircraft
Investigation
Recap/Notes:

THE AIRCRAFT INVOLVED, N4713U, was a 1970-vintage Boeing 747-122. She was the eighty-ninth jumbo jet Boeing built and made her first flight from Boeing's Everett plant at Paine Field on the October 20th, 1970.

United took delivery soon after and put her into service on November 11, 1970.

February 24, 1989, she was eighteen-and-a-half years old and had accumulated 58,815 hours over 15,028 flight cycles. In that time, there hadn't been any significant incidents or damage—although there was a fairly typical history of age-related corrosion, fatigue cracks, and the engine troubles that plagued all early 747s.

In fact, the airplane had lost its number three engine on short finals into Honolulu, just days before the accident flight, on February 17, 1989—this time due to a false engine fire warning triggering an automatic shutdown. (In a strange twist, the crew would get no fire indications from the number three or four warning systems on the 24th, despite visible fires coming from both engines.) —*Excerpt from "Airscape Magazine," www. airscapemag.com*

September 26 and October 1, 1990: The cargo door was recovered in two pieces from the ocean floor at a depth 14,200 feet.

During the initial NTSB investigations into the cargo door malfunction, it was initially thought to be human error in closing the door, and the NTSB was looking into the final cargo door closing procedures executed by the United Ramp Agents. One ramp agent was particularly emotionally affected, as he was the final person to close and lock the door. This United employee suffered enormous stress and guilt until the NTSB proved that the cause was an electrical malfunction, not human error.

Flying shrapnel and debris damaged the right wing's leading-edge devices, denting the horizontal stabilizer on that side and striking the tailfin.

NTSB reported human remains and pieces of clothing in the number three engine.

The probable cause of this incident is a faulty switch or wiring in the cargo door control system.

A design flaw in the cargo door locking mechanisms and a lack of timely corrective actions by Boeing and the

FAA following a cargo door opening incident on a Pan Am 747 in 1987 also contributed to this malfunction.

The Pan Am incident led Boeing to issue a service bulletin detailing modification for the latch locking systems on cargo doors.

January, 1990 was the deadline to complete the work, and United had not yet applied the relatively modest $3,027 modification cost on this aircraft at the time of the incident.

This incident became known as one of the most shocking cases of a known design flaw being ignored by the airlines. The FAA gave airlines just thirty days to comply following United 811.

The aircraft was successfully repaired at the reported cost of $14 million, then returned to service with United Airlines in 1990. In 1997, it was registered with West African Air Dabia, a Gambia-based airline until abandoned in 2001. In 2004, the plane was put out of service, now utilized only for parts.

For further information and photos on the repair process of the most devastated 747 that had ever returned safely to an airport, refer to the Airscape Magazine article "United 811, The Untold Story".

https://airscapemag.com/2017/02/08/

United Airlines ran recreations through their flight simulator. Despite many attempts and variable tweaks, they were unable to successfully land an aircraft after losing the forward cargo door.

A 747's estimated cruising speed at 24,000 feet is 350–400 mph. In comparison, the highest recorded hurricane wind is Hurricane Allen at 190 mph. The highest recorded tornado is 1999 in Moore, Oklahoma, at 301 mph.

Flight deck crew: Captain David Cronin, First Officer Al Slater, and Flight Engineer Randal "Mark" Thomas.

Cabin crew members: Purser Laura Brentlinger, Aft Purser Sarah Shanahan, Ricky Lam, John Horita, Curt Christensen, Tina Blundy, Jean Nakayama, Mae Sapolu, Robin Nakamoto, Ed Lythgoe, Sharol Preston, Ricky Umehira, Darrell Blankenship, Linda Shirley, and Ilona Benoit.

Passengers Lost: Anthony and Barbara Fallon, Long Beach; Harry and Susan Craig, Morristown, NJ; Lee Campbell, Wellington, New Zealand; Dr. J. Michael Crawford and John Swan, Sydney, Australia; Rose Harley, Hackensack, NJ; Mary Handley-Desso, Bay City, Michigan.

Captain Cronin was on his final round trip flight before his mandatory retirement. He envisioned routine flights to and from Sydney, then going home to enjoy the next chapter of his retirement life. A few years after the incident, it was time to keep my promise to myself to buy the captain a beer.

After Mother-Vic had relocated to the Denver area, she mentioned she always wanted to meet and thank him. She and I flew to Reno to enjoy lunch with Captain Cronin and his wife near their home on the shores of Lake Tahoe.

From there, Captain Cronin and I stayed in touch over the years with annual Christmas cards and talked now and again. He was grateful to hear the passengers' version and happy to share his cockpit experiences. A humble and sincere man, Captain Cronin experienced a major heart attack and died October 6, 2010. He was eighty-one.

In 1989, Transportation Secretary Samuel Skinner awarded the pilots and cabin crew the Secretary's Heroism Award, citing that the flight attendants overcame "the deafening, hurricane-like winds that swept through the cabin" as they helped passengers deal with the crisis over the Pacific.

In a separate meeting, the Airline Pilots Association bestowed Superior Airmanship Awards to Captain Cronin, First Officer Slater, and Flight Engineer Thomas.

An accurate recreation of an explosive decompression is the airplane crash scene in the opening of the movie "Castaway".

February, 1989. The aircraft on the tarmac at Honolulu International Airport.

February, 1989. Showing the damage.

February, 1989. Photo taken during the incident at 24,000 feet, approximately 100 miles from Honolulu. You can see my head in the lower left hand corner as I am reaching across the aisle to hold the arm of the passenger in the damaged seat. Photo courtesy of passenger Martin Bastock. Even though Martin was seriously injured with a significant left elbow and arm break caused by a runaway beverage cart, he bravely managed to take photos during the incident, just in case...

February, 1989. Actual emergency evacuation on the Honolulu tarmac. Passenger Martin Bastock took this photo as I am about to exit the aircraft via the evacuation slide.

February, 1989. Early morning post evacuation scene on the Honolulu tarmac. Photo courtesy of Martin Bastock.

February, 1989. The aircraft being inspected for damage on the Honolulu tarmac. This photo shows the investigator standing in the damaged area of the missing seats of rows 8-12. The passengers seated in the two seats shown just past the open floor are the passengers I was attempting to hold on to as their feet dangled out the hole.

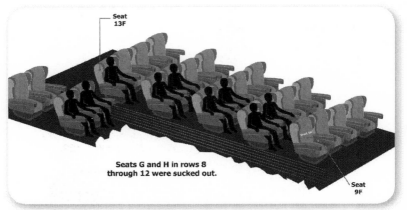

United 811 seating chart showing the window and aisle seats (seats G and H) in rows 8-12 that were suctioned out of the aircraft. Also showing is the location of Seat 9F, my originally assigned seat and Seat 13F, where I was seated.

February 28, 1989. The Sydney article showing me looking out the window of my hotel room. This is where I would sit when I needed to gather myself, look out at the "normal world" going on around me and remind myself I would be back there some day. I had not slept in something like 60 hours at this point.

March 7, 1989. The Front Page of the Rocky Mountain News. My long time friend and co-worker, Muriel Benjamin, would not let go when greeting me upon my return to Stapleton. Courtesy of The Denver Public Library, Western History Collection, Call Number WH2129.

February 24, 1989. The Front Page of the Honolulu Star-Bulletin. Courtesy of the Honolulu Star-Advertiser.

About the Author

SHARI PETERSON WAS RAISED in a small rural Iowa farm community of fewer than 400 residents. While Shari and her two younger sisters were growing up within the community's humble lifestyle, they witnessed their parents demonstrate that "small town, helping others" philosophy by donating and contributing to their school, church and community.

Following the life altering event of United 811 in February 1989, Shari began her quest for understanding her own life. She began traveling extensively sharing her experiences and teaching personal development. One of her discoveries was her ability to effectively communicate and counsel people, empowering them to greater personal growth.

Shari has appeared on *Oprah*, *Turning Point*, *Hard Copy*, *Angels II Beyond the Light*, *I Survived a Disaster* and *It's a Miracle*. Shari has been featured in magazines and appeared on TV and radio in the US, Europe and Australia.

After nearly 30 years of gentle nudges from people all over the world to write this book, Shari is now ready and willing to share this, her first publication.

While this effort has been an enormous learning experience for Shari, she hopes her readers will recognize similar struggles in their own lives and be inspired to embrace their authentic selves.

Using Shari's favorite self-talk starter, "Hey, this is going to get fun!", her wish is that her readers can confidently move forward, ready to handle anything while making new, bold choices.

Shari shares her experiences, and life lessons from United Flight 811 in speeches around the country. To book Shari for your event please contact her through ShariPetersonAuthor.com.

Made in the
USA
Middletown, DE